Counting the Cost:
The Economics of
Christian Stewardship

Robin Kendrick Klay

William B. Eerdmans Publishing Company
Grand Rapids, Michigan

Library of Congress Cataloging-in-Publication Data

Klay, Robin Kendrick, 1947-
  Counting the cost.

  Includes index.
  1. Economics—Religious aspects—Christianity.
2. Christian ethics. I. Title.
BR115.E3K523 1986   261.8'5   86-16212

ISBN 0-8028-0171-4

ACKNOWLEDGMENTS

Figure 1 on p. 82 is found in *Pollution, Prices and Public Policy* by Allen V. Kneese
and Charles L. Schulz (Washington: The Brookings Institution, 1975), reprinted
from Clifford S. Russell's "Restraining Demand by Pricing Water Withdrawals
and Wastewater Disposal," in *The Management of Water Resources in England and
Wales* (Saxon House, 1974). Used with permission.

Figure 2 on p. 83 is found in *Pollution, Prices and Public Policy* by Allen V. Kneese
and Charles L. Schulz (Washington: The Brookings Institution, 1975), reprinted
from Clifford S. Russell's *Residuals Management in Industry: A Case Study of Petroleum Refining* (Baltimore: The Johns Hopkins University Press for Resources
for the Future, 1973). Used with permission.

The fable about protectionism that begins chap. 8 is taken from Frederic Bastiat's
Economic Sophisms, trans. and ed. by Arthur Goddard (New York: Foundation for
Economic Education, Inc., 1975). Used with permission.

Tables 1 and 2, found on pp. 129 and 130, are reprinted from Michael C.
Munger's "The Costs of Protectionism: Estimates of the Hidden Tax of Trade
Restraint," in *World Trade and Trade Finance* (Albany: Matthew Bender, 1985).
Used with permission.

Contents

Preface

This book was born out of two economists' frustrations over the absence in sermons and Christian publications of any great appreciation for how economies function, what motivates and rewards economic behaviors, and why meeting the material needs of humankind requires a willingness to face difficult economic choices and their anticipated outcomes. My colleague, Jim Heisler, joined me in the initial dialogue and plans for a book which would help clergy and lay Christians fill this void. He also authored Chapter Three.

As the book progressed, others assisted mightily with the birthing process. Chief among them was Cory Pepoy, an inspirational and meticulous reader of early drafts. At other stages Tom Ten Hoeve, Dan Ebels, and Jim Heisler also were helpful critics. During its final stages, editor Mary Hietbrink smoothed the delivery in ways that amazed and delighted me. Technical assistants in the "delivery room"—Joy Forgwe, Kathy Dykstra, and Amy Van Es—did much more than type the manuscript. They cared for me and expressed hope and delight over the emerging creation. In fact, the entire Hope College community is to be credited for the intellectual and financial support they have provided me. In addition to thanking these people for their supremely creative and competent contributions to this book's development, I wish to thank Kathie Spitzley and Lori Knap, whose loving care for my son, Nathan, during the months of writing made me a grateful believer in a modern extended "family."

May the efforts of these people be rewarded by the Creator in whom and for whom all our hopes and labors have meaning far beyond these printed pages.

For which of you, desiring to build a tower, does not first sit down and count the cost, whether he has enough to complete it?

Luke 14:28

Counting the Cost

CHAPTER ONE

Introduction: Christian Faith and Economic Knowledge

> Most readers are not known for their economic sophistication. Many have avoided the "dismal science" . . . and are therefore unable and unwilling to go after their economic analysis firsthand.
>
> Robert Benne
> *The Ethic of Democratic Capitalism: A Moral Reassessment*

Several years ago, when I was teaching in Cameroon, West Africa, my sister took a break from medical school to visit me. Although her clinical background was limited, her offer of help was eagerly accepted by a mission hospital, where she was immediately put to work performing both diagnoses and surgery. She soon became uneasy about the very large numbers of people who were being adequately treated but inadequately educated about their treatment. Patients left the hospital knowing as little about the rationale behind their Western-style treatment as they did about the various means employed by native healers. Consequently, many patients ended up back at the hospital with complications that could have been avoided if their own basic intelligence (and that of their families) had been enlisted in their recovery and health maintenance.

Like the medical personnel trying to help the Cameroonians, many people have engaged their hearts and wills in the search for solutions to social ills. But these solutions must be based on understanding sufficient to avoid high costs and ephemeral cures. Christians everywhere are being challenged to bring their faith to bear on current social issues. Sermons take us to task for living in relative ease while neighbors, near and far, starve. Books challenge us to exercise more responsible stewardship of the earth's resources to counter environmental degradation. Theological studies tell us either that American-style free enterprise is God's will for every society, or that revolution and socialism are God's plan to liberate the oppressed and unite the human family. All too often we find ourselves assaulted with recitations of distressing problems and then asked to accept a set of purportedly straightforward, biblically informed answers. But where is the prudent, intelligently informed analysis of these complex problems? Can we really jump, unaided, from a sprinkling of raw data to simple solutions?

The overriding purpose of this book is to enlist readers' intelligence as well as their hearts and wills. It attempts to bridge the gap between a faithful desire to find solutions to social-economic problems and the frustrating complexities of these real-life issues. Sometimes complexity paralyzes people who want to solve problems. This book is based on the premise that a knowledge of economic logic, coupled with Christian faith and values, can produce effective solutions to which people can commit themselves and their resources. One of the main purposes of this book is to identify the costs (and the unintended consequences) of important social measures to help the poor, protect workers, and safeguard the environment. A bold look at costs can actually serve as a solid foundation for courageous responses to problems. In assessing costs we are forced to do some clearheaded thinking about personal, social, and spiritual values.

I became an economist for reasons very much linked to the purposes of this book. While I was growing up in the 1960s, issues of civil and economic justice were publicly debated. My parents saw to it that these issues became family concerns and provided a focus for lifetime commitments patterned after Jesus' own life with and for the dispossessed. Although I did not expect economics to interest me, my first college course in the subject was enough to persuade me that the study of economics is crucial to devising effective personal and collective responses to poverty and to a whole range of other social issues. I learned that the economist's intellectual tool-kit is invaluable for assessing the material implications of various proposed solutions to problems, and for identifying the most efficient means to achieve goals which themselves might largely transcend materialism. Furthermore, I appreciated the economist's ability to help people identify the *costs*—financial and otherwise— of undertaking any given action.

The economist accepts scarcity as *the* fundamental and pervasive economic problem. From this starting point he or she proceeds to analyze the implications of scarcity for the private and social choices we all make about how best to use our time, money, and other resources. One of the economist's self-appointed tasks has always been to help people make their choices explicit and to clarify for them the likely results of their choosing (even unintended results). As a college student, I began to see that the tools of economics were essential to fulfilling a commitment to Christ in the world. Agonizing social problems can be neither understood nor effectively dealt with until scarcity and its implications are taken into account. As Christians, we recognize that scarcity is simply the economic dimension of human finitude. Not all good things can be simultaneously had or accomplished because our lives and resources are finite. On this side of heaven we have to choose, and we want to choose intelligently. Such a perspective may pose unique challenges for Christians. Some believe that Jesus' miraculous feedings of thousands could be replicated on a much grander scale if Christians had sufficient faith. To them the assumption of scarcity is either faithless or false. But if Christians could transcend the mundane limitations of scarcity by faith alone, as this stance suggests, we would have no need for economic logic. Establishing priorities among the good things we want to see accomplished and choosing the best strategies to meet those ends would not be a problem. Our greatest need would be to correctly apprehend God's purposes and then tap into his limitless resources. But in a fallen world the faith that can move mountains entails stewardship of that which is so scarce we dare not waste it. The faithful are called to exercise both faith *and* stewardship.

The Bible is replete with stories about people who were called to undertake great tasks that required them to prudently plan their use of personal and communal resources. The Bible also tells of living faith, which was sometimes honored by God with miraculous provisions of entirely new avenues and resources. By faith Abraham answered God's call to leave Ur with his entire household. He took along provisions for sustaining his family on their journey—something that required planning and making decisions about what to leave behind. This great patriarch exercised similar prudence when facing subsequent challenges. When a famine occurred in Canaan, Abraham wisely fled to Egypt. When he and his nephew Lot returned to Canaan, the two separated because the land could not support both of them and their families. Such necessary husbanding of limited resources does not appear to compete with Old Testament calls to faith but rather to complement them. If lifted out of context, some teachings of Jesus that urge us not to be anxious about the future might seem to break with Old Testament teaching. The whole of Jesus' teaching, however, appears to call for both prudent, nurturing stewardship *and* faith. Indeed, in several parables Jesus uses the example of a shrewd, energetic, income-generating steward in order to encourage the seekers of the Kingdom to assert similar energy and wisdom in pursuit of their higher goal.

Like the steward, we are called by Jesus to bold action grounded in faith and guided by knowledge. Accordingly, this book describes the tools of economic analysis, and explains how they can be used in the light of Christian faith and ethics. Scarcity forces us to choose, and God calls us to make well-intentioned *and* well-informed choices because of our love for him and his creation. If it is based on knowledge and faith, choosing can be an exercise in faithfulness.

The next two chapters examine the nature and necessity of economic choice wherever private and social wants outstrip available resources. The advantages and limitations of markets as devices for managing scarcity are compared with the claims made for alternative economic arrangements. The remaining chapters are devoted to key issues—such as poverty and environmental degradation—that lend themselves to economic analysis and also have important moral dimensions. The aim of each chapter of application is to explore the facts, understand the economic forces at work, examine the policy options available, and link all these to the teaching of Scripture. No single "Christian" answer is offered for any of the complex problems raised. The goal is to explore the costs of each option so that our choices can be more astute and also more faithfully obedient as God's priorities are permitted to illumine our values.

Most of the issues dealt with in this book are the stuff for which shocking facts can be revealed, threatening scenarios written, and revolutions incited. The quotations at the opening of each chapter suggest how heated are the debates, how passionate the concerns. The outcome of this investigation into the economics of Christian stewardship should prove to be less sensational yet ultimately more satisfying and engaging than the extreme positions with which many a genuine quest for truth has begun.

An Exercise

Inventory your initial concerns about many economic motivations, activities, and structures by examining your reactions to the common economic terms below. Reflecting on the list may reveal your own passions and prejudices. It may also uncover some contradictions—for instance, you may note that while cooperation is normally a good thing, in the form of monopolies or cartels it can lead to the exploitation of the many by the few.

Rate each of the terms listed below from 1 to 5 based on the degree of their compatibility with the teachings and practice of the Christian faith (1 = not very consistent; 5 = very consistent). Take note of any possible contradictions among your ratings for different terms.

competition	rewards
cooperation	capitalism
exploitation	socialism
profit	economic growth
incentives	speculation

conservation
insurance
saving
risking
calculating

trust
equality
collective
business
nonprofit

CHAPTER TWO

Scarcity—The Fundamental Economic Problem

TANSTAAFL: There Ain't No Such Thing as a Free Lunch
Title of a book on environmental economics by Edwin G. Dolan

Socialist criticism of capitalism was in fact a criticism of the human condition, that is, of the central problem of scarcity, with which socialism would have to cope just as did capitalism.
Henry W. Spiegel, *The Growth of Economic Thought*

Economic reasoning begins with scarcity, a nagging fact of human existence. While scarcity is usually equated with shortages, it has a different meaning in economics. Something is scarce if it can be acquired only at some cost—that is, there is not enough naturally available, or producible with human effort, for everyone to freely have his or her fill. When people want apples, nightly news, or even clean air badly enough to pay a price for them—however low the price—these goods are scarce. Actually, no money need change hands. If I am willing to forego any good thing in order to obtain any other good or to ensure that some service is performed, that good or service is said to be scarce. It is the scarcity of this good that forces me to make a choice. The pervasive problem of scarcity is so important that this entire chapter will explore how scarcity forces choices upon individuals, groups, and whole societies.

SCARCITY AND ITS IMPLICATIONS FOR INDIVIDUALS

Imagine a Garden of Eden untroubled by scarcity. In such a place the inhabitants can eat all varieties of fruit in any quantity they like simply by plucking them from the trees. Because their supplies are abundant, their energies inexhaustible, and their days endless, these people need not decide who gets what. Even if the particular type of fruit desired is not available in their present location in the garden, a trek of one thousand miles to acquire it will never be a problem. What is a forty-day journey in a life whose days stretch out forever?

This brief glimpse of an Eden is sufficient for us to appreciate that the most fundamental scarcity we all face outside of the Garden is finite time. Because our days are not endless, we care about how much time and effort might be required to satisfy our wants. In addition to the fundamental scarcity of time, we who live this side of Eden face scarcity of material resources to supply our wants. The story of Robinson Crusoe provides us with a good illustration of this. Crusoe may have had to do virtually no work to merely survive, but in order to clothe himself decently by European standards and to enhance the quality of his life in other ways, he had to use available resources—those he scavenged from the wreckage of his ship as well as those already on the island. Thus he frequently confronted scarcity of means relative to a multiplicity of wants. Furthermore, he had to choose carefully among those means in order to husband his time and energies to satisfy several types of wants. (The word *need* is not used here because it implies the absence of substitutes, whereas economics most often is about the choices we make among substitutes.)

In order to make his initial stock of bread from the ship last longer, Crusoe limited himself to eating one piece a day while he made certain agricultural tools that would later improve his ability to provide sustenance for himself. For several years he set aside all his corn and barley crop to use as seed until he could expand his production sufficiently to provide for current consumption and future plantings. Both of these acts we recognize as forms of saving (which usually take a monetary form today), which in themselves directly indicate a person's response to current scarcity of resources relative to future wants.

Besides undertaking these "economizing acts" to manage his food resources, Crusoe also thinned his dwindling supply of ink in order to prolong its usefulness for the keeping of his daily journal. This record-keeping was certainly not a necessity for life, but it was one of many endeavors that Crusoe undertook to increase his personal comfort. During his later years on the island Crusoe chose to sacrifice additional comforts in order to take measures to protect himself from the natives who began visiting the island for cannibalistic feasts.

What we learn from the Crusoe story is that, besides the fundamental scarcity of time, we all live with scarcities of basic resources. This is true whether we live alone on an island and contend with only our own wants, or live together in a society where others' wants may clash with our access to resources. Just as Crusoe was unable to avail himself of resources on nearby islands, so we are limited to retrievable resources in this neighborhood or nation, on this continent or planet by the available technology, as well as by other factors such as politics and income. (Of course, technology—that is, the knowledge and ability to make commercial use of resources—evolves over time. Futurists are now contemplating the day when we will be able to extract mineral resources from the moon or other planets. Our plans to meet resource demands in the near future, however, treat the earth as the sole source of supply.)

Raw resources usually have to be transformed by work into usable commodities and tools to perform services. Those who will do the work, whether solitary Crusoes or individuals living in society, must decide how to allocate their time among the various activities of training, working, and consuming. Crusoe was forced to be a self-sufficient unit: he had to raise his own crops, bake his own bread, and perform all his own domestic chores. Keeping his overall satisfaction in mind, he carefully decided how much time he could "afford" to spend on each activity. But even when we live in society and can delegate certain chores of maintenance to others, the limited amount of time we have forces similar choices upon us. Both for Crusoe and for us, each bit of time has value. We cannot afford to use our days and years with complete abandon.

THE IMPLICATIONS OF SCARCITY FOR PEOPLE LIVING IN SOCIETY

Our own lives differ from Crusoe's because of the complexities associated with life in society. We are not self-sufficient producers, so we have to rely on mechanisms that coordinate our efforts with those of others, enabling us to trade for what we do not produce ourselves. The goods and services that we produce with finite personal time, energy, and natural resources are not so abundant as to be free for the asking. This basic scarcity forces us to make choices in our role as consumers. Most of us cannot eat T-bone steaks every night or get daily medical checkups because to do so would require us to give up other good things, like a warm house or a good book.

Thus scarcity of time and resources forces each of us to make choices regarding production and consumption. This side of Crusoe's island, scarcity in the real world also makes for competition or outright conflict among individuals and groups over access to that which is scarce. No matter how their economy is organized, people compete for top athletic honors, good jobs, and admission to very popular concerts. Societies differ in their approach to resolving the question of how to fairly and efficiently allocate both the incomes with which scarce goods and services can be bought, and the goods and services themselves. Selfishness aggravates the allocation problem. But even without it, the scarcity of good things would still set the stage for competition among those who wanted them.

What is true for individuals this side of Eden is also true for groups of individuals organized into families, churches, voluntary organizations, businesses, and governments. None escape the fact of scarcity, which results from collective aspirations exceeding the limited means available to achieve them.

FAMILIES

Each family faces limitations on its ability to produce or trade for goods and services to supply its wants. Family members must choose what amounts of hamburgers and video games, or steaks and canoe trips, will provide them with the best overall level of satisfaction. If a family is very wealthy, they might easily exhaust their taste for material luxury yet not escape the need to confront other types of scarcities such as scarcities of time, status, and power. For instance, a family consisting of two medical doctors and their children may feel no need to make careful budgetary decisions about their spending on fancy groceries, fine clothes, and expensive cars and boats. But time constraints may "force" them to choose maid service and brief luxury vacations rather than the more time-consuming joys of domestic tasks and leisurely family trips. Or suppose for a moment that the Voss family is independently wealthy and is therefore able to devote nearly all of their time to consumption rather than production. It still doesn't take long to think of several areas in which the Vosses might have to make economizing choices about the use of scarce resources. They may be interested in achieving prominent social status or the power to influence people, either in their own self-interest or for the sake of others. Because there is not an unlimited amount of status and power to satisfy all those who desire them, we can expect competition to ensue over the means to acquire them. Is it a yacht, a private tennis court, or a lavish gift of a building to their alma mater that will best guarantee a rise in their status? Obviously, the answer depends in part on what other status-seekers might be doing. If the power to influence others is the goal, the family must first consider the most economical route to a given degree of power. Subsequently, they may want to "invest" power they have already achieved in the way best suited to increasing it.

CHURCHES

What we have said about competition over access to scarce material and social resources and about economizing choices in their use is applicable to all units of society. Consider a church that may have the highest motives. It will not be spared the agony of choosing whether a thousand more dollars should be spent on the education of church youth, the local food bank, evangelization, or foreign relief projects. Because of its limited budget, its decision to support any one project is clearly made at the expense of other legitimate tasks.

GOVERNMENTS

Sooner or later all individuals and groups bump up against the hard rock of scarcity—including governments. Since the mid-1970s we have seen that even a very wealthy government will eventually confront a scarcity of financial resources in attempting to meet a plethora of public wants. In the 1980s the necessity of choice has become clearer. Taxpayers have balked at rising taxes, and the economy itself has ceased to grow at rates that would make rising government expenditures comparatively painless. Under such circumstances, the need to choose between B-1 bombers and aid for the helpless produces acute social distress. We realize more than ever that scarcity forces us to clarify our social values. How much will we pay for a bomber, a school, clean air, safe cars, Social Security, foreign aid? These are questions that must be answered in terms of what we are willing to give up to meet a multiplicity of socially desirable aims.

SCARCITY, CHOICE, AND COMPETITION— PROBLEMS THAT TRANSCEND MOTIVES

In Chapter One the point was made that there is no real conflict between our accepting the fact of scarcity and living in faith. In a similar vein, we should consider to what extent scarcity and all it entails are products of impure motives.

Does a selfless monk with few material desires face scarcity and participate in the scramble for resources? At the most basic level of time and physical energy, this monk faces the same types of problems as anyone else. With twenty-four hours in his days and an unknown but limited number of days at his disposal, he must carefully decide (in the context of a religious community) how to get the most out of those hours for the sake of God and his neighbor. No matter how simple the monk's personal needs for physical maintenance, his ability to produce will be scarce relative to the number of good things he will feel called upon to do with his time—hence the need to choose which people he will help and to what extent. He will share in the all-too-human pain of knowing that choosing to spend one dollar or one hour for the sake of Alice implies the willing sacrifice of an opportunity to do the same for John.

Besides having to make choices, even a monk will be forced by scarcity to compete with others for the right of access (by purchase or otherwise) to goods and services. If he trades or sells cabbages to support himself, his order, and their charitable concerns, he will want to produce cabbages without duplicated or otherwise unproductive efforts, and to sell them for the higher of any two prices offered him (all other things being equal). By doing so, he will be a good steward of the finite resources at his disposal, and he will be able to use the returns for his presumably enlightened and spiritually informed priorities.

Scarcity can, of course, be aggravated by grasping selfishness. Clearly, selfishness can so distort the allocation of scarce goods that some people are denied their right to live with dignity—or their right to live. But the fact remains that scarcity is not eliminated by good motives. Though loftiness of motive may distinguish our monk from an unrepentant Scrooge, both individuals must cope with scarcity by making costly choices and competing with other producers and consumers.

SUMMARY

Scarcity in some form impinges on all of us. It is tempting to reason that there must be a solution to the problem of scarcity by way of induced or forced reduction in levels of wants—a favorite suggestion of philosophers, kings, and certain religious groups. But it is the claim of this book that human beings this side of Paradise will be forced on several fronts to face up to the absolute necessity of choosing among competing goals precisely because the means are too scarce to achieve them all. Each of us must decide how best to use and conserve time, energy, and resources—how best to "economize." And that means we must analyze costs and values, as economists do. Thus economic analysis comes into play whether or not money is involved. And it is equally applicable to both individuals and groups, to both the poor and those who are materially well-off. Economic analysis is an especially crucial skill for Christians who have been called to cope with the demands of both Caesar and God.

Questions for Further Consideration

1. Economists treat scarcity—the gap between our material wants and our ability to supply them—as a given. A Christian might add that scarcity is a "post-Fall" condition, and therefore partly a result of sinful human choices made by us and by our ancestors. Of course, acute scarcity can be mitigated by increasing production, redistributing income or goods to the most needy, and curbing wants. Is any one of these ways of dealing with scarcity more Christian than another?

2. All churches struggle to be faithful stewards of their limited financial resources. Every year requests are gathered from various church groups who want resources to fulfill their responsibilities. Throughout the year many special requests for additional funds come from groups and individuals within and without the church. Does your church (or other service organization) have a satisfactory way of clarifying what is being sacrificed when it decides to fund activity X (and thus leave activities Y and Z undone)?

3. In Luke 14:28 Jesus said we should "count the cost." When we do this, our values are often laid bare. For instance, I might decide that arranging for my grandmother to visit will entail foregoing the purchase of some personal or household equipment. Making this choice and then living within the resulting material limitations may remind me of how much I love my grandmother. Can you think of any personal or collective choices that were improved and perhaps made less painful by "counting the cost"?

CHAPTER THREE

Social Responses to the Problem of Scarcity

by James B. Heisler

[Economics] shows clearly that under highly competitive conditions, profitability and production of products most wanted by society exactly coin-
cide. This coincidence of profits and satisfaction of wants (and needs) is the
genius of the market system.

Paul Morgan, "Is Capitalism Christian?"
La Paz: The Westmont College Magazine

After broadening my horizons, I became convinced that, in respect not only
to horses, but to all things, this notion of "my" and "mine" is nothing more
than a low, primitive human instinct which they call the sense or right of
private property. There are men who say "my house," yet they've never
lived in it; "my land," yet they've never walked on it; "my people," yet they
do their people harm.

Strider, the horse in the musical *Strider* by Mark Rozovsky

Moral rhetoric is very close to the surface in the theory of socialism whereas
the moral values of democratic capitalism are much less visible.

Robert Benne
The Ethic of Democratic Capitalism: A Moral Reassessment

Scarcity is a problem for everyone. Each individual must deal with the
problem because it is a condition of human existence. But human beings
are social animals. We work and play in groups; we organize our activities together in ways that adapt and respond to the conditions around
us. As groups, we face the same constraint of scarcity that we face as
individuals. In fact, much societal organization springs from the need to
address the problem of scarcity. Customs, laws, and government both
structure and enforce social responses to scarcity. For instance, they
determine the ground rules for the ownership, use, and exchange of
property, as well as rules for the exchange of human services. All this
would be unnecessary if human and physical resources were unlimited.

Scarcity forces all social organizations to answer three fundamental
questions: What? How? and Who? Let us deal with each of these in turn.

Scarcity means that we can never have everything we want. Consequently, we must decide *what* among the myriad of things we want we
will actually produce. This is true for both individuals and societies. An
individual's limited income may not allow him or her to have one house,
two cars, three square meals a day, a fashionable seasonal wardrobe, a

home computer, a color TV with cable channels, and expensive charitable interests all at the same time. The choices made among these things will reflect the individual's preferences and values.

Similarly, societies must choose what will be consumed collectively. The limited resources available to the people of a society can be used to produce numerous things designed to be social goods: roads, hospitals, schools, education, bridges, public beaches, statues, missiles, police forces, fire protection, space shuttles, post offices, and opera companies. It is essential to understand two important aspects of this social "what" decision. First and most obviously, choices must be made among these social goods. Second and perhaps more fundamentally, resources devoted to the production of social goods will not be available for the production of goods to satisfy individual consumer wants. Thus the satisfaction of social wants reduces our ability to satisfy private wants. Viewed another way, the social "whats" must be added to the list of private "whats" from which an individual must choose. How does an individual choose a social "what"? The political structure of the society in which he or she lives must provide a vehicle for directing resources from private to public production and a means for determining what is "appropriate" social production. In Western democracies, for example, taxation transfers resources from the private to the public sector, and bodies of elected officials decide how these resources will be used.

The second fundamental question that scarcity forces us to answer is "how"? Once it is determined what, in fact, we will produce, we must choose a way of producing it. There are usually numerous ways to produce anything or achieve any given end. Determination of the method to be used involves consideration of the available techniques or technologies, the quality and prices of materials to be used, and the "appropriateness" of the method. Should tomatoes, for instance, be produced using pesticides or "natural" insect controls? Should they be harvested by machine, which requires planting a variety with uniform maturity rates and thick skins to avoid bruising? Should containers be made of light aluminum, cheap paper or plastic, or recyclable glass?

Decisions about "how" clearly are made by individuals and family units as well as businesses. In a society in which the productive activity of individuals is exchanged for some payment that will then be used to acquire the "whats," the first "how" question is, "How will I allocate my time and other resources to acquire the skills I will use in the production process?" The second question is, "How will I produce the income that will be used to purchase the goods and services on my want list?"

The "how" decision of production requires every business to determine how it will bring resources together to make a product. Individual workers and businesses must answer questions about "appropriateness." Is any way to make a dollar acceptable? Are some ways to make a profit legally acceptable but morally questionable? While producing something for the lowest possible cost may be a favorite and successful answer to the "how" question, is it always the way that ought to be chosen? Customs and mores enter into these decisions, and different individuals and institutions answer these questions differently. Slavery provides "cheap" labor. Lakes and streams provide "cheap" dumping grounds. Prostitution is the "oldest profession" and may be highly remunerative. Caveat emptor—"let the buyer beware"—is profitable if the seller is not interested in repeat sales.

Societies, however, may determine that these and some other answers to the "how" question are not acceptable. Thus they may prohibit certain activities and require others. Laws in this country prohibit slavery, prostitution, and false advertising. Laws also make mandatory such things as equal pay for equal work, minimum wages, and certain degrees of waste treatment. These controls take the form of legal constraints, but societies also affect the "how" question by establishing fundamental structures and rights (such as private-property rights). Even the absence of legal controls is in some cases a societal answer to the "how" question. The result may be reliance on tradition or on a set of common values. No matter what constraints are imposed—legal or traditional—productive activity does occur. When it does, the "how" question has been answered.

"Who" is the third fundamental question raised by scarcity. Once productive activity takes place, the question of distribution—of who is to get what—arises. Before he met Friday, Robinson Crusoe had little difficulty in answering the "who" question: he got everything that was produced. But the addition of another person, the beginning of a societal arrangement, forced him to make a fundamental decision about the distribution of the fruits of their efforts. Family units must also make these decisions. "How much spending money will Daddy have?" "Can I have an advance on my allowance, Mom?" "We'll all have to make sacrifices if Peter goes to college." These are all distributional issues that must be addressed in the microcosm of the family. Similar distributional decisions must also be made in larger social units such as nations.

Other distributional issues arise from the employer-employee relationship. In economies in which the input of employees may be only one part of the final product, and perhaps not a visible one at that, how much of the value of that final product will each employee get? We who are employees may all think that we get too little and the "boss" gets too much, but what we do get is an answer to the question of "who." How the output in a society is distributed, then, is a social question. It depends on the arrangements agreed upon by those who exchange income for productive effort or resource use. Here again, however, these arrangements may be constrained by social decisions. The minimum wage and time and a half for overtime hours are familiar examples of socially established distributional arrangements. Societies may also be involved in redistributing output independent of work effort. Some goals such as a minimum standard of living, the elimination of great disparities in income, and distribution of all output on the basis of need rather than productive input are examples of social responses to the "who" question on a broader scale.

Finally, it is important to note that the way in which the "who" question is answered has direct implications for the answers to the questions of "what" and "how." Individuals spend their incomes in different ways, so in a trivial sense any redistribution of income is likely to result in different "whats" being produced in a society. Widespread redistribution from the very affluent to the very poor, however, is likely to result in a much more fundamental rearrangement of the "whats" produced in a society, since the goods and services the two groups buy are significantly different. We would expect more small suburban homes and fewer mansions, more economy cars and fewer luxury cars, more hamburgers and fewer steaks to be demanded and therefore produced. In a similar way, any redistribution of income that affects the price that employers must pay for factors of production (land, labor, and equipment) will affect the combination and the quantity of production factors that will actually be used—that is, "how" production will take place. It may also affect the incentive to produce or offer factors of production for sale in the first place. A significant redistribution of income from the rich to the poor would, for example, increase the demand for low-cost housing. This in turn would cause the wages of carpenters to rise. Consequently, contractors producing homes might try to economize on increasingly expensive skilled labor by using more and more prefabricated materials. At the same time, the higher earnings of carpenters would likely draw more skilled workers into that employment. In this way a change in the answer to the "who" question feeds back into the questions of "what" and "how."

It is clear, then, that every society must deal with these three fundamental questions. Every society and social organization is different in the details of its response. Nevertheless, it is possible to broadly categorize social responses to these questions in a way that will give us insight into the nature of the economic orders around us. In one sense, this is a study of the economic "isms": capitalism, which depends heavily on markets, and socialism, in which answers to the questions of "what," "how," and "who" are determined by governments.

A MARKET SYSTEM

INDIVIDUAL TRANSACTIONS

One way a society can organize its economic relations is to allow markets to generate the answers to the fundamental questions. The term "market" refers to the coming together of people who want to buy something with people who want to sell something. The mechanisms for conducting these transactions may be simple or complex, involve few people or many, but the essence of a market is voluntary exchange. Potential buyers come to a market with a demand—a sense of what they are willing to buy under certain circumstances. In similar fashion, potential sellers come to a market with a supply—what they are willing to sell under certain conditions. The interaction of this supply and demand, which results in a voluntary exchange of goods for goods or goods for money, is the market outcome.

As Americans, most of us are familiar with market transactions. We engage in them every day when we buy a loaf of bread, pay our rent, buy or sell a share of stock, or accept a job for a particular wage. Indeed, our experience makes it difficult to envision doing things another way; the market seems like the natural order of things. This is deceptive, however, because in much of the world people are not allowed to engage openly and freely in market transactions. In these places the market is not the legal means by which people acquire the things they want, and sometimes they resort to trading in the black market. To understand societies that are organized around a market economy as well as those that are not, it is necessary to thoroughly explore the workings of markets and explicitly examine the nature of the outcomes under this form of economic organization.

All markets require some objective standard by which the value of the product to the individuals involved may be measured. That standard is *price*. The price both indicates the amount of money needed to conclude the exchange and provides essential information to the participants in the market. To potential buyers, the price is an indication of the magnitude of sacrifice necessary to conclude the transaction. If a pizza has a price of seven dollars, a potential buyer knows that buying the pizza means not buying seven dollars' worth of other things. Those other things represent the "opportunity cost" of buying the pizza. With this information in hand, Jackie, a potential buyer, can determine if the pizza is "worth it." Note that price does not convey anything about the inherent value of the product. Thus, while a pizza lover like Jackie may think that a pizza for seven dollars is a bargain, Nathan, who is nauseated by the sight of any combination of tomatoes and cheese, may find fifty cents an exorbitant price and be unwilling to pay it. To potential sellers, the price indicates the value of materials that can profitably be drawn into production of that good or service.

Price, then, is the key link between buyers and sellers in a market. When the buyer and seller agree on a price that is beneficial to both, an exchange will take place. Two important points must be made about this exchange. First of all, it is voluntary. Either party is free to accept or reject the price. Second, by implication, both parties are better off after the exchange than before it. If they had not anticipated this outcome, they would not have made the exchange in the first piace. (Of course, mistakes can be made. Buyers and sellers can underestimate or overestimate the value of a good to them. If this happens, however, they will be better prepared to engage in the next transaction and will not conduct it on the same terms.)

A market system consists of a very large number of these individual transactions. Many people are seeking to buy and sell many products and services. All of these interactions order the economic life of a market economy. We will see that the fundamental questions of "what," "how," and "who" are automatically answered in the markets themselves.

THE MARKET RESPONSES TO THE FUNDAMENTAL QUESTIONS

What is produced in a market economy? The obvious response is that things that are demanded will be produced, but we must be careful here. The willingness of *some* people to spend *some* money on *some*thing is not sufficient to ensure its production. If it were, the Ford Motor Company would still be producing Edsels. On the other hand, far fewer people buy Ferraris today than were buying Edsels the day that production of that car ceased—yet Ferraris are still being produced. Demand isn't the only thing that matters, then. The key to what is produced in a market economy is *profit*. Very simply, a profitable item will be produced; an unprofitable item will not be. And something is profitable when the revenues from the sale of what is produced exceed the costs of production to an extent sufficient to encourage someone to produce.

At this juncture it is crucial to understand the function of profit in a modern market system. Profit is typically a reward given to individuals or groups who provide the financial capital to make certain productive activities possible. Just as workers offer their services for a reward (wages) and land and property owners offer their resources for a reward (rent), owners of financial capital expect a reward for investing their money in an economic venture. Production cannot take place without the financial resources to rent buildings or build a plant, buy the necessary equipment and materials, pay the workers, and so on. As long as the production process is carried on with private ownership of the means of production, that production will not take place in the absence of the expectation of profit. A producer's refusal to commit financial resources to a project without good prospects of making a profit is, therefore, no different from a worker's refusal to offer labor if no wage is offered him. Both wages and profits are vital to the production process, and both rewards are necessary if production is to take place.

Profit, then, is a reward, but it also functions as an allocator. In a market economy, the rate of profit directs the flow of resources and thus directs production. The greater the number of people who demand something, the higher the price of the product. The higher the price, given the costs of production, the more profitable the production of the item, and the greater the volume that will be produced. The less people want of something, the less they will spend on it, and the lower the price of that item will be. If that price does not allow the producer to make as much profit producing that item as can be made producing some other, he or she will stop producing it. Thus people in a market economy get what they really want (as evidenced by their willingness to spend money on it) and don't get what they don't want. Ferraris and matches will be produced if they are profitable. On the other hand, Edsels and pet rocks will not be produced if they stop being profitable.

Profitability is also the key to a market economy's answer to the "how" question. Quite simply, the method of production chosen will be the one that generates the highest rate of profit for the producer. Thus the producer will choose more productive inputs (land, labor, and equipment) over less productive ones and lower-priced inputs over higher-priced ones. The resulting production is described as "efficient" because it results in a product of a given quality being produced at the lowest possible cost. Here, as with the "what" question, we find profit performing a dual function. As a reward to producers, it affects the particular way any good or service is produced. The competitive nature of the reward system also ensures that production will take place in an efficient, low-cost way, a definite benefit to consumers.

Finally, the market system also answers the "who" question. In a market system, the goods are distributed to those who can afford to buy them—people with income. Individual income is generated by the sale of labor, property, or financial resources in the marketplace. The resources and services that command the highest income are those that are in the greatest demand. If a lot of people want to pay to watch football and there aren't many good football players, football players will earn a high income. If people are not very interested in rugby, then rugby players will be likely to have a lower income. Thus the big "who's" in the marketplace—those able to buy what they like because of their high incomes—are the people who are willing and able to offer their services to suppliers of those items produced most profitably in the marketplace.

In summary, then, the market system answers the fundamental economic questions automatically. A society organized around such a system needs no central authority to make these decisions, no central information-processing unit, and no communal ownership of resources. It does need laws and law enforcement to support the system of private ownership and market transactions, but otherwise the system is self-governing. The actions of consumers, workers, and business owners in the marketplace are conditioned by their moral and ethical judgments, good or bad; morally motivated constraints are not imposed on these actions from outside the system. The sum of these actions determines, to a certain extent, the answers to "what," "how," and "who." Nevertheless, the extent to which the market is allowed to answer the fundamental questions varies greatly from society to society, and few if any have ever allowed the market free rein. To understand the basis for collective constraints on the market, we must understand how certain market solutions would lead to results that might be regarded as unsatisfactory by large segments of society.

POTENTIAL SHORTCOMINGS OF A MARKET SYSTEM

A society that accepts the market form of economic organization may also determine that some of the results of the normal workings of the market are unsatisfactory, or inappropriate to other social goals. While these shortcomings are often referred to as "market failures," the degree to which they are deemed unacceptable depends on the attitudes of people in the society. These attitudes may be based on moral principles and are thus the concern of Christians everywhere. It is important to understand that the concept of a "market failure" implies that the society is not universally in agreement with the market outcome. If everyone were to feel and act in the same way, the market would respond appropriately, and no market failure would occur. For instance, if everyone in a society agreed that prostitution was inappropriate and therefore no one demanded it, the market would not support this activity because it would not be profitable. The social problem arises when not everyone in a society agrees about the appropriateness of a market outcome, thus allowing the market to support some level of an activity deemed inappropriate by certain people. Let us examine, then, some categories of market outcomes that are frequently objected to by many members of societies because they dislike the market's answers to the fundamental questions. Specific discussions of many of these problems and corrective policies will comprise the remaining chapters of this book.

THE "WHAT" PROBLEM: SHOULD PEOPLE GET EVERYTHING THEY WANT?

A virtue of the market system is that it provides consumers with what they want as long as it is profitable to do so. Frequently, however, large segments of the population regard certain commodities or services as undesirable. Most people in the United States, for example, regard heroin as a product that should not be available for purchase. Nevertheless, enough people want it to make it profitable to sell it. It is so profitable, in fact, that sellers are willing to bear the high costs of avoiding law-enforcement authorities and a high risk of being caught. We can all think of commodities or activities that we believe should not be offered in the marketplace. But it should not surprise us to discover that our lists would vary considerably. Alcoholic beverages, marijuana cigarettes, hand-guns, pornographic movies, slot machines, and abortions—all these are examples of goods or services that some people would outlaw and others would not. In a society where individual freedom is highly valued, the philosophical problem is that placing constraints on such goods and services reduces that freedom. The practical problem is that market forces remain strong when moral forces are too weak to eliminate demand for the objectionable item. Americans learned this lesson with the failure of Prohibition to eliminate markets for alcoholic beverages.

THE "HOW" PROBLEM: SHOULD PEOPLE BE ALLOWED TO PRODUCE IN ANY WAY THEY WANT?

The pressures of the marketplace encourage producers to combine their inputs in the least costly manner, thus maximizing the profits to be made. If these lower production costs are passed on in the form of lower prices, the consumer benefits. This process also ensures that the relatively scarcest productive inputs (reflected in the higher prices of goods produced with them) will be conserved. At the same time, however, this process may lead to certain outcomes and activities that are socially undesirable.

In production that results in waste materials, for example, the cheapest way of disposing of that waste is to dump it, perhaps in a nearby body of water or into the air. It is no geographical accident that chemical plants have typically been located near large bodies of water. A pipe running from inside a plant to a nearby river is a very inexpensive means of waste disposal. The result is a low private cost of production for the business. The problem is that the cost of waste disposal has not disappeared; it has simply been externalized, passed on, in a different form, to a different group of people. Those who use the water for recreation may find the fish dead and the water too polluted for swimming or boating, and so may spearhead clean-up campaigns. Those who depend upon it as a source of water supply may find that additional processing is needed before the water is potable. These are all "social" costs, because they are borne by society rather than by the individuals involved in the market for that product.

Pollution, then, is one example of a "how" that society may wish to constrain. Other examples abound. If a business is free to choose whatever employees it likes, should it also be free to refuse employment to certain groups of people because of their race, sex, or religion? If the wage is determined in the market, is there any wage that should be regarded as too low? If the technique of production presents a certain hazard for employees, should it be allowed as long as these employees are willing to accept the danger? In any of these and other circumstances, a society may choose to modify the market answer to the question of "how."

THE "WHO" PROBLEM: SHOULD PEOPLE HAVE TO WORK BEFORE THEY CAN EAT?

The market rewards those who respond to market forces. This built-in incentive is a strong inducement to working hard and responding to the signals of the market. If the market provides the only source of income for an individual or a family, it is also a very strong disincentive to sloth and the production of things with little market value. Contrary to the expectations of the Protestant work ethic, however, hard work and good intentions are not always sufficient for market success, nor are they always necessary. People who are unable to participate productively in the market will have little or no income. This means that the market does not reward the people whose mental or physical handicaps reduce the marketability of their skills. People who possess outdated skills will be treated similarly. Even the possession of skills or resources that are in great supply relative to the demand for them will result in a lower market reward. Discrimination is also a factor. If society at large decides that blacks or women will only be allowed to perform certain kinds of jobs and expresses that decision in marketplace actions, all the hard work and good intentions in the world will not make the railroad porter an engineer or the saleswoman a company president.

The arbitrariness and insensitivity of the market in relation to human subsistence has given rise to several attempts to alter such market outcomes—for example, direct government income supports, subsidies for necessities like housing, minimum wages for workers, and agricultural price supports for farmers. Alternative ways to address the income problem will be examined in Chapters Four and Five.

COMPETITION

The responsiveness of the market to consumer demand and to changes in that demand rests on the willingness and ability of individuals to produce in accordance with the market dictates by responding to the profit motive. The condition that ensures this "willingness and ability" is competition. When the competition is strong, no single firm or group of firms is able to affect the market outcome independently. Individual firms find themselves responding to market circumstances, not creating the circumstances. However, even Adam Smith, the eighteenth-century "father of economics," realized the great desire of business competitors to reduce the rigors of the competition. He observed that "people of the same trade seldom meet together, even for merriment and diversion, but the conversation ends in a conspiracy against the public, or in some contrivance to raise prices." This is the desire to acquire monopoly power, the leverage over prices that comes with market control. With this kind of leverage firms can dictate to the market rather than serve consumers' best interests. Over time they can earn excessive profits, which in a competitive market is a signal for other firms to enter the industry and meet the market demand. Monopolists are those producers who succeed in preventing any such invasion of their profitable corner of the market.

Thus competition is good in a market economy—indeed, it is essential for the economy to work properly. But in a market economy there is also an incentive for individuals to eliminate competition in order to improve their own situation. This fundamental contradiction is the subject of public policy in market-oriented economies. In the United States, antitrust laws and regulations have been attempts to deal with the problem of maintaining the benefit of competition without eliminating the stimulus to respond creatively and actively to market forces.

THE PUBLIC GOODS PROBLEM

As we have seen, the market system will respond to any set of demands that makes production profitable. Individuals demand goods and services for which they will receive benefits exceeding the price they must pay. For example, I will buy a green polo shirt if the benefit I receive from it exceeds its price. The shirt I buy and wear may provide some enjoyment to passersby, but I am most concerned about my personal enjoyment of it—its color, its comfort, its versatility—when comparing expected benefits to cost.

But there are some goods and services that convey substantial benefits to many people simultaneously in such a way that no individual can be effectively excluded from those benefits. When certain individuals pay for the service and others can enjoy its benefits at no cost, many of these beneficiaries will be unwilling to pay their contribution to its production. (Consider the campaigns to persuade "freeloading" viewers of public TV to send in contributions.) These goods that provide benefits to many people, none of whom can be excluded from the benefits, are often called "public goods."

With public goods, the market simply does not automatically translate and transmit the individual-benefit information into effective market demand. National defense is a good example of a public good. Most people in the United States believe that they derive some benefit from a military system that provides a defense against nuclear attack. Very few of these people, however, could afford to buy that protection themselves. And most would be reluctant to make voluntary contributions to pay for national defense if nonsubscribers would enjoy the same protection as subscribers. Of course, once a defense umbrella is provided, it is extremely difficult to exclude nonbuyers from the benefits. Consequently, an economy based totally on a market form of organization would not find this kind of good emerging from the market.

Most people recognize the existence of public goods, which raise a difficult question: What goods should qualify as public goods, and how shall they be financed? It is relatively easy to say that national defense is a public good, for example, but what constitutes national defense, and how complex a defense system is appropriate? Similar questions can be asked about flood control, roads, police and fire protection, airports, public parks, education, and health care. The market answers many fundamental questions, but it is mute on the subject of public goods.

THE BUSINESS CYCLE PROBLEM

The market is a self-regulating system that responds to the actions of individuals. Businesses produce the quantity of goods and services that are profitable for them. The total level of output for the entire economy is the sum of these individual market transactions. If, for whatever reason, people in the economy spend less on goods and services, businesses will produce less. This in turn means that fewer workers will be hired by individual businesses, and unemployment for the entire economy will rise. At this point the "multiplier effect" comes into play: when people lose their income, they naturally buy less, and this leads to greater unemployment. This cycle is not easily broken.

When each producer is producing the amount that is profitable at that point in time, the economy reaches an equilibrium, a position where no further change automatically occurs. But this equilibrium is not necessarily positive; it may occur when there is massive unemployment in the economy. At the depth of the Great Depression, for instance, the U.S. economy was very probably in equilibrium. The market system provides no automatic correction for this phenomenon.

In similar fashion, the economy can overheat when individual spending outstrips the ability of firms to produce. The result is higher prices in individual markets and inflation for the economy as a whole.

This "business cycle" problem is really the problem of overall economic instability in a market economy. There is nothing inherent in a market system that prevents the economy from going through large swings in the overall level of economic activity. The history of the U.S. economy prior to World War II is one of such wide swings. And even if a market economy, like a pendulum, always swings back from an extreme position, societies may raise questions about the cost such swings exact in human suffering and lost output. Attempts to ameliorate such swings have characterized economic policy in most industrialized market economies since the Great Depression.

ALTERNATIVE RESPONSES TO THE FUNDAMENTAL ECONOMIC PROBLEM

Societies that are fundamentally market-oriented have long wrestled with the above shortcomings and altered the market in an attempt to produce more satisfactory outcomes. In general, the way markets are modified depends upon the society's evaluation of the nature and severity of the problem and the likely impact of potential modifications. This, in turn, is a reflection of the attitudes, values, traditions, and moral codes of the society. A society that does not traditionally value and honor the role of the elderly, for example, may be relatively unwilling to modify the market to prevent age discrimination or to ensure financial security for the aged. In the same way, a society that views business organizations as nonthreatening vehicles for achieving economic success will be less likely to impose constraints on their market behavior.

Modifications such as the antitrust laws designed to prevent monopolies and ensure competition actually attempt to strengthen the market. Other modifications use the market to achieve given ends, allowing the market to function but under certain kinds of restraints. Minumum-wage laws and agricultural price-supports improve the incomes of the sellers in the markets. Gasoline taxes assist in encouraging consumers to reduce consumption and conserve a specific resource. Other modifications eliminate the market completely. Public goods such as public education, freeways, and national defense are provided to all citizens in the United States on a nonmarket basis—that is, without consideration of each beneficiary's ability and willingness to pay what it costs to produce the services he or she enjoys.

Modifying market conditions is an element of the continuing struggle to improve the lot of individuals within societies. The market system is not sacrosanct, however. Some socialist societies believe that the struggle of production is best dealt with outside the context of markets, and they reject the market system. They view capitalism—a highly charged term for a market-dominated economy based on private ownership of the means of production—as a system that works to the benefit of a few, encourages antisocial behavior, promotes racism and sexism, rewards domestic and international exploitation, and alienates workers from normal relations with each other and the environment.

THE COMMAND SYSTEM

Once the market is rejected as the means to answer the fundamental questions, an alternative system must be adopted. It is important to note that the fundamental economic problems and questions do not disappear with the removal of a market economy. If the questions are not to be answered automatically in the marketplace by independent individuals acting in their own self-interest, then the answers must be imposed on the people of the society. Decisions must be made centrally and carried out through authority, essentially by command. This does not necessarily imply that many individuals are not participating in the decisions or that a democratic process is not involved in the choice of those who make the decisions. But it does mean that some decision-making authority must decide exactly what is to be produced, how it is to be produced, and who will get the fruit of the production.

Most of us have firsthand knowledge of this type of economic organization, because it is the typical model of American family life. The issues of occupations, allowances, meals, bedtimes, family chores, and movie selection are usually not resolved on a supply-and-demand basis. The lion's share of clothes, food, and toys do not go to the child able to earn the most money. And some jobs like washing dishes are usually rotated rather than being permanently assigned to the person who does the fastest and the best job. In fact, considerations of equity and need rather than of productivity loom large in many of these family decisions. In this system, the greater production abilities of some family members compensate for the handicaps of other members. And because any shirkers in a small, close-knit system can be dealt with by disapproval, families need give little thought to the fact that a widespread system of guaranteed shares in resources weakens incentives for individual effort.

Such an economic system may have distinct advantages, being particularly strong in those areas where a market system is weak. A principal advantage of this system is its ability to control the distribution of income. This is the basis of the "command economies" of most socialist and communist countries. Rather than allowing the vagaries of the market to determine an individual's claim on the means of subsistence, a command economy may simply determine the "best" distribution of the nation's output and carry it out. The scheme involved would vary. It might be based on equal distribution of every product, or it might be based on the Soviet Union's creed: "From each according to his abilities, to each according to his needs." The extremes of absolute poverty and excessive riches could thus be rapidly abolished.

Other problems arising in the market system could be dealt with in a similar fashion. Since production in a command economy is determined by a central authority and not subject to the condition of profitability, socially undesirable products would not be produced (even if some social deviants wanted them). In addition, the method of production would not have to be the most profitable and could thus be one most consistent with other social objectives such as a clean environment, community development, and equal-opportunity employment. Thus the command economy—in theory at least—provides the most direct vehicle for achieving socioeconomic goals while avoiding the onerous aspects of market organization.

WEAKNESSES OF THE COMMAND SYSTEM

A command economy in which the decision-making authorities accurately respond to the goals and wishes of the people in the society can also avoid many of the inefficiencies of market organization. The market system is a confluence of many indirect signals. In essence, people's desires are compared with prices, and spending decisions are then made. Producers must decide if production is profitable and what the most profitable form of production is. If they are to produce an item, how much is too much or too little? What if they raise or lower the price of their product? What if they change the product slightly? How should it be advertised? These are only a few of the calculations and decisions made. Trial and error is a distinct part of this process. As with military maneuvers and sailboat races, the shortest distance between two points is reached when not everyone is a general or a captain. In a command economy, production decisions can be made and consequent actions taken directly. A free-market system with comparatively limited government intervention might have produced great engineering feats and gotten Americans to the moon, but Sputnik was the product of a command society.

Despite its advantages, however, a command economy is not without its political, ethical, and economic shortcomings. While a command economy is not necessarily totalitarian (since decision-makers may be elected and even certain decisions may be made through an electoral process), it does limit individual free choice in many areas. Minimizing the conflict between the individual's self-interested economic actions and the society's well-being is at the heart of Communist-Marxist analysis of and response to the market system. The consequent limitations may affect people's choice of jobs, their consumption alternatives, and what they are permitted to own. Some economists (like Nobel prizewinner Milton Friedman) argue that when economic freedoms are limited, political freedom is jeopardized. Any evaluation of a command economy must include the implications of this trade-off of lesser individual freedom for potentially greater communal welfare.

The command economy also has some purely economic shortcomings. First is the problem of information and coordination. In a market economy, price and profit are carriers of information about relative scarcities, and decisions about "who," "what," and "how" are based upon this information. In a command economy, which rejects this function of prices and profits, something must be substituted for it. While this is seldom a problem for a household making family decisions, it is a significant problem when the organized unit is an entire society. Many thousands of products are produced using millions of workers and billions of productive inputs. Should Jane Doe be used as a laborer tightening bolts numbered 59, 60, and 61 on tractors in Gdansk, or should she take notes in the district court in Krakow? Should glove compartments in cars be made with coin holders or with glass holders? Or with both or neither? Should the goods produced be what individuals in society want? If so, how will those wants be conveyed, and how will they be ranked? If goods are to be distributed by handing them out, who will get what? If they are to be sold at a price, what is the "correct" price? Should the price paid by the consumer be tightly linked to the production cost incurred by the producer, or should the two diverge, as they frequently do in the Soviet Union? The problems of information and coordination for large economic units are obviously staggering.

A second economic problem typical of command economies is one of incentive. Within the limits of a market economy, greater effort is rewarded with greater economic reward. There is a direct and personal incentive to work hard, train for the kinds of jobs in demand, and respond to market forces. If a command society adopts a method of distribution in which reward is not based upon this kind of performance, the problem of incentive may arise. Will workers and producers do their best when they will get the same economic return by doing less? This is essentially a question of human nature. Many people in Communist economies argue that the "true" nature of human beings is to work for the good of the whole society rather than the good of the individual, or at least to identify the good of the individual with the good of the whole. This natural inclination, they say, is thwarted and perverted by the imposition of a capitalist market economy on the workers.

While definitive conclusions about human nature are difficult to reach, the evidence from modern economies around the world suggests that productivity does increase when it is rewarded. Even in the People's Republic of China—the object of perhaps the purest large-scale experiment in Communism to date—increased emphasis is being placed on individual rewards for productivity in what is called the "responsibility system." This raises the question of the trade-off that may exist between equity (some measure of "fairness" in income distribution) and efficiency (some measure of productive responsiveness). This trade-off is not unique to command economies, but they must deal with it if productive efficiency is a desired societal goal. When private and social wants far exceed available supplies, productive efficiency will usually be an intermediate goal.

CONCLUSIONS

In their pure forms, both market and command economies represent extremes in societal attempts to deal with the fundamental economic problem. Most of the world's economies operate between these extremes. The degree to which either markets are allowed to function freely or collectivities are given the power to command frequently depends on the particular problem being dealt with (e.g., how many cars to produce or "how much" education to provide), the level of organization responsible for it (families, cities, or nations), the homogeneity of culture and values in a population (e.g., multi-ethnic American or substantially mono-ethnic Scandinavian), and a myriad of other factors.

As Americans, we face a diversity of social problems— ranging from protecting the environment from chemical ravages to meeting the needs of the poor—that have distinctly moral dimensions. Understanding the most appropriate responses to these problems requires us to know both the facts of the problem and the costs and benefits associated with alternative solutions. Allowing economic considerations to come into play does not imply that one's moral position must be compromised, but rather that to make a truly moral judgment, one must be adequately informed about the economic realities.

Questions for Further Consideration

1. For generations, some people have questioned the morality of profit. Marx is well-known for maintaining that profit is exploitive because it goes to people who do not work. The argument presented in this chapter accords an important dual role to profit: first, it functions as a reward to those who at some risk provide the financial resources needed for production; and second, it functions as a device that draws resources into ventures that are highly valued by consumers. How do you feel about this justification of profit?

2. There are probably some products or services that you believe the market should not supply. If you are in a group, try comparing your individual lists. Which is the best approach for dealing with this problem—persuading people not to buy the product or service, protecting the people who are particularly vulnerable to the appeal of this market (such as youth), or banning the good or activity altogether? Does your choice of

approach vary depending on the item—e.g., heroin, prostitution, abortion, gambling? At what point is the safeguarding of freedom of choice a value that you are willing to sacrifice to some other value?

3. What has been the special moral appeal of socialism to many Christians? Read the Benne quotation at the beginning of this chapter. Are the moral and practical claims made for free markets equally as persuasive? What do the strengths and weaknesses of each suggest to you about the wisdom of or need for a blend of the two?

4. Should the size and complexity of a social unit (e.g., family, church or club, firm, town, state, country) reasonably affect our choice to allocate resources by collective decision or to leave the task of resource allocation to markets?

CHAPTER FOUR

Poverty in the United States

> The patrimony of a poor man lies in the strength and dexterity of his hands; and to hinder him from employing this strength and dexterity in what manner he thinks proper without injury to his neighbor, is a plain violation of this most sacred property.
>
> Adam Smith, *The Wealth of Nations*

> These labourers, who must sell themselves piece-meal, are a commodity, like every other article of commerce, and are consequently exposed to the vicissitudes of competition, to all the fluctuations of the market.
>
> Karl Marx, *Manifesto of the Communist Party*

> The poor-laws of England were undoubtedly instituted for the most benevolent purpose, but there is great reason to think that they have not succeeded in their intention. They certainly mitigate some cases of very severe distress which might otherwise occur, yet the state of the poor . . . is very far from being free of misery.
>
> Thomas R. Malthus, *An Essay on the Principle of Population*

Poverty. What is it, and what are its causes? What progress, if any, has been made in its alleviation? What more ought to be done about it, and at what cost? These are burning questions for anyone of conscience. Perhaps they are even more rightfully troubling for Christians, whose Scripture reveals again and again the concern that God has for the plight of the poor. Ron Sider's popular book, *Rich Christians in an Age of Hunger,* is one of many in recent years that have called on the world's affluent Christians to radically change their own life-styles and seek to effect changes in economic institutions in order to achieve greater justice for the poor. Faced with such proposed solutions, Christians need to become better informed about the facts of poverty and more familiar with various explanations of its existence and propagation if they hope to evaluate and participate in the best answers to the problem. In this chapter we will examine what economic analysis reveals about the causes of poverty in our own country and evaluate some attempts at alleviating it. The international dimensions of poverty will be considered in the following chapter.

INCOME DISTRIBUTION—WHY ARE THE POOR "ALWAYS WITH US"?

The Bible says that the poor will always be with us. Economic analysis can explain how the poor came to be among us in the first place, and why a redistribution of wealth does not in itself eliminate the problem.

IS POVERTY A MATTER OF CHOICE?

An explanation of the overall income distribution that evolves in a largely market-oriented economy simultaneously explains both wealth and poverty. It tells us why the economic pie is divided up in such a way that some individuals receive more personal income from their labor and property than do others. Conservatives begin by assuming that individuals exercise considerable freedom in determining what their subsequent incomes and wealth (or poverty) will be. After all, an individual may choose lengthy and expensive training or short and inexpensive training; he or she may select an occupation, a location, an employer, and the number of hours worked per week, each of which implies a certain level of income. Beyond that, individuals are also presumed to decide whether and how much to save out of current income in order to provide for themselves at some time in the future.

According to this explanation of income distribution, janitors, waitresses, and a large number of the poor who do not hold paying jobs at all are poor because they opted against education and training, failed to save or acquire assets for a more secure future, and chose to spend time at home rather than in the work force. Similarly, doctors, successful entertainers, and business executives earn high incomes because they chose grueling studies, years of low-paying "gigs," and minimal family life.

Most of us would not have nearly as much concern for the poor if we believed this story to be the whole truth. However, we know that routes to poverty or wealth are not always rationally chosen, but instead result from cumulative good or bad fortune for which the individual is not responsible. Perhaps the janitor was from a poor black family and could not choose to attend college because of extremely limited means and crying family needs, which required that she/he find work immediately after finishing high school. Or maybe at the time she/he was thinking about future employment, janitoring and similarly low-skill jobs were all that blacks could reasonably aspire to in Mississippi or Watts or Detroit. The waitress may have suffered other social disabilities that severely restricted her options. If she was married and had a family, she may have been expected to go wherever her husband's best job prospects were and to find a job with flexible hours that would allow her to provide most of the child care. A person without any paying job might be staying at home because high unemployment rates and low-level skills (and perhaps employer prejudice) severely limit his or her possibilities for getting a job. In addition, jobless persons and others may be poor because of physical or mental handicaps that don't allow them to work at jobs highly valued by the market. Even the individual who makes a well-informed and conscientious decision to train for a certain occupation may subsequently be disappointed by low pay or no job at all simply because market conditions have shifted dramatically since the time he or she began job training.

On the other hand, the doctor may have gotten through medical school because his or her parents were able to afford a prep school that virtually assured successful entry into an elite college and medical school. The now popular and rich entertainer may be no more talented than the average aspiring star, but may have been blessed with extraordinary physical beauty or had the right connections because of the family name.

Thoughtful consideration of our own lives and those of others suggests that conscious choices with respect to training, career, willingness to work hard or take risks, and even levels of saving and avenues for investment represent only a partial explanation for the incomes that people enjoy or suffer under. Indeed, all too often, factors over which we have little or no control have been significant determinants of our financial success or failure—such things as gender, family wealth, religion, the luck of circumstances, and changing market conditions. Nobel prize-winning economist Paul Samuelson sums up the unpredictability of economic rewards in a line from *Economics from the Heart:* "When we see a friend in the line for unemployment compensation we each say, 'There but for the grace of supply and demand, go I.'"[1]

This absence of a perfect link between effort expended and income rewards received should give rise to certain misgivings about a completely noninterventionist approach to poverty and lead to social attempts to deal with this problem.

WOULD REDISTRIBUTION OF WEALTH ELIMINATE POVERTY?

Those who greatly appreciate the workings of competitive markets for their efficiency in meeting consumer demands often fail to acknowledge explicitly that the resulting income distribution depends heavily on how

---

1. Samuelson, *Economics from the Heart: A Samuelson Sampler,* ed. Maryann O. Keating (San Diego: Harcourt Brace Jovanovich, 1983), p. 5.

evenly wealth and other advantages or handicaps are initially distributed. Let's imagine that, to avoid this problem, some ethnically homogeneous society redistributes nonhuman assets (money, real estate, stocks, etc.) such that all persons share equally. For a short time this will guarantee a sort of "equal starting point" in a market-dominated economy and thereby re-establish a stronger degree of personal responsibility for decisions regarding education, occupation, and effort that together lead to an array of different incomes. For a time it can be said that the gap between poor and rich in this society is substantially voluntary and hence of no great ethical or social concern. But it will not take very long for unmerited income gaps to appear because of "bad luck," poor parental decisions that leave certain children several steps behind the equal starting point, or depressed markets for certain skills. These gaps will be further widened by the unmerited advantages of others.

Perhaps it is because we can expect the recurrence of unmerited income gaps and certain injustices that the Bible records in various places, "The poor will never cease out of the land" (Deut. 15:11). Although this statement may sound pessimistic, it is followed by a positive "Therefore, I command you, You shall open wide your hand to your brother, to the needy and to the poor in the land." This should not be interpreted as solely a call to personal charity; the Mosaic law goes on to specify certain specific obligations owed to the poor by individual Israelites and the whole nation of Israel. These included the right of the poor to glean at harvest time, the liberation of slaves during every seventh year, and the return of all lands to their original owners during every fiftieth year (called the Year of Jubilee). Thus the Old Testament Scriptures called for institutionalized as well as personal correctives to be regularly applied to income distribution. Nowhere does the Bible seem to question the legitimacy of rewards for effort; indeed, it frequently proclaims these to be good. On the other hand, it explicitly denies that the poor generally deserve their poverty (or that riches are always a sign of righteousness), and calls upon people of faith to devise ways to regularly meet both the current needs of the poor and their need for an opportunity to start over again, using new resources to productively support themselves.

If we can expect that most market-dominated economies will periodically leave all sorts of people in the stagnant backwaters while the mainstream rushes on, then Christians face a divine mandate to consider what are the best means for both dealing with the immediate distress of the poor and restoring them to the possibilities for economic dignity and freedom available in the mainstream. A comparison of means must deal with the potential costs of each one—in the form of both direct material costs and lost opportunities. After all, even Jesus berated the tower builder not because his goal was foolish but because he forgot to "count the cost" (Luke 14:28-30).

The classic conservative answer to this question has always been "Let those of the well-off who are so moved give alms to the poor." This is the basis for all kinds of charitable giving that is channeled to the poor in the form of direct income gifts, in-kind support (clothes, housing, education, tools, and so on), and even new opportunities to earn a living. Recently this argument for private charity has been supplemented with a popular conservative call to vastly reduce levels of government involvement in the economy. Welfare reform, deregulation of product markets, an end to minimum-wage laws, and a flattening of tax rates would supposedly promote economic growth. A larger economic pie, to some extent, would automatically be shared with the poor. A supplementary benefit of these proposed changes would be the creation of incentives inducing and enabling the poor to improve their lot by more active and productive participation in the economy. These changes would thereby also reduce paternalism and increase opportunities for the poor to exercise responsibility for their own choices about earning and spending. But what conservatives decry—significant government intervention in the economy—is precisely what liberals have taken pride in because of its contribution toward reducing U.S. income disparities in general and poverty in particular.

To understand this issue more fully, it is necessary to examine the pattern of change in the U.S. distribution of income and the incidence of poverty in the United States, and to explore the likely explanations for these changes.

THE CHANGING CONDITION OF THE POOR IN TWENTIETH-CENTURY AMERICA

WHAT HAS HAPPENED TO INCOME INEQUALITY AND THE FREQUENCY OF POVERTY?

Most studies of the *distribution of income* in the United States since the late 1800s show that few trends were noticeable prior to 1929, but that between 1929 and 1950, income equality improved substantially. A measure often used to depict how equally income is distributed among members of a population is the "income concentration ratio." If everyone were to receive identical incomes—the case of "perfect equality"—the ratio would be 0. If only one person received all the income and the others received none—the case of "perfect inequality"—the ratio would be 1.

By this measure, income inequality gradually fell from .488 in 1929 to .371 in 1948. After 1950 there was no clear further drop in income inequality, but measures that attempt to incorporate nonmonetary public transfers (such as medical assistance, food stamps, housing assistance, job training, and education) into the distribution of income point to further decreases in inequality. By one estimate, the share of total income received by the poorest 20 percent of the U.S. population rose from 8.1 percent in 1952 to 11.7 percent in 1972.[2] (At the opposite end of the spectrum, the share of after-tax income going to the richest 20 percent of the population decreased from 36.7 percent in 1952 to 32.8 percent in 1972.)[3]

Government studies that zero in on the *incidence of poverty* in the United States rather than income distribution point to specific progress made against poverty until the late 1970s. These studies define poverty ac occurring when household income falls below the estimated dollar income necessary to meet minimum standards of nutrition, housing, clothing, and so on. The dollar figure varies according to family size and is adjusted annually to reflect changes in the cost of living. According to census statistics, the percentage of Americans living in poverty fell from 22.4 percent at the beginning of President Johnson's "war on poverty" to 12.6 percent in 1970, but then ceased to fall further after that. However, according to the Congressional Budget Office, once adjustments are made for most in-kind benefits (such as food and housing subsidies), the rate of poverty in the United States dropped to 6 percent of the population in 1976.[4] Other studies estimate the percentage fell as low as 3 percent.[5]

2. Edgar K. Browning, "How Much More Equality Can We Afford?" *The Public Interest* 43 (Spring 1976): 90-110.

3. A variety of legitimate criticisms can be made of the particular way that nonincome transfers (such benefits as food and housing subsidies) were added to income to derive this optimistic view of recent improvements in the distribution of income in the United States. For instance, nonincome benefits were valued at their market prices rather than at the value (undoubtedly less than their price) which the poor themselves attached to these particular goods and services. Many people who accept "free" cheese from a state or government distribution program, for instance, would buy something else if they had the money equivalent to its price. Because the valuation of benefits is a sticky question, we should probably interpret the data that point to an increased share of total income going to the poor as indicative of only *some* continued movement toward equality since 1950, but not a great change.

4. Robert Paul Thomas, *Macroeconomic Applications: Understanding the American Economy* (Belmont, Cal.: Wadsworth Publishing, 1981), pp. 83-86.

5. For example, Morton Paglin's 1979 study, cited by Thomas in *Macroeconomic Applications*, p. 86.

Thus data on both changing income distributions and the incidence of poverty defined in terms of a dollar benchmark suggest that the poor have made gains since the Depression. Although measurements of the changes vary, it still appears that those gains have come more slowly since 1950. Since 1979, measured income inequality and poverty have worsened both because of a long recession and because of reduced welfare coverage under the Reagan administration. Wendall Primus, chief staff economist for the House Committee on Ways and Means, estimates that between 1979 and 1984 the rate of poverty (after payment of taxes and receipt of benefits) increased for all individuals by 40 percent and for families with children by 64 percent. If federal and state government welfare policy had remained unchanged since 1979, there would have been about five million fewer poor (after benefits) in 1984. According to Primus, changes in government policy can explain approximately 52 percent of the recently rising poverty rates for families. (The rest has to do largely with the recession and changing family structures.) A similar story can be told about worsening income distribution over the same period. In what follows we will return to the prior period of gains against poverty in order to put into perspective the recent historical role that government policy has played (or failed to play) in the battle against poverty.

WHAT CAUSED AMERICANS' INCOMES TO BECOME MORE EQUALLY DISTRIBUTED?

To what can we reasonably attribute the gains that have been made against inequality in this century? Are they a product of changes in the economy at large, or the result of direct policy measures on behalf of the poor? A variety of factors are responsible for the rather dramatic improvements between 1929 and 1948, but it is difficult to assess the relative importance of each. Over this period the share of income paid for labor services (i.e., wages and salaries as opposed to capital income paid to owners of financial and physical property) rose from 59 percent in 1929 to 64 percent in 1950. (Since 1970 it has remained constant at 75 percent.) This rise in labor's share of income occurred partially because of a slower influx of immigrant workers, whose numbers had previously been so great that unskilled laborers could not effectively bid for higher wages.

At the same time that growth of the unskilled labor force slowed, rapid improvements were being made in the average worker's education. This "human capital" enhanced earning powers of the labor force, as would be expected from the accumulation of any valuable capital asset. Because labor incomes are more equally distributed than capital incomes (and have become more so in this century), and because the share of all income paid to labor has also risen, overall income equality in the United States has improved.

Since 1929, generally lower rates of unemployment have also contributed to greater income equality in that the incomes of low-wage workers have been better protected against involuntary job loss. Jobs and incomes have been protected because for several decades the federal government has taken direct responsibility for establishing and exercising fiscal and monetary policies to prevent recessions from getting out of hand. In addition, those who have lost their jobs temporarily have been protected from destitution by unemployment insurance. News reports on the increased incidence of poverty during the recession of 1980-1982 reminded us of poverty's link to the cyclical—boom and bust—nature of a market-oriented economy, and of the importance of using federal policy to promote high employment levels.

It is popularly believed that minimum wage laws and unions have also contributed much toward income equality and the fight against poverty. But the constraints of supply and demand suggest that neither minimum wages nor union wage demands can exercise any significant role in affecting poverty. For instance, studies on the impact of minimum wages on the distribution of income show that their impact is small, in part because many low-income workers (e.g., teens) are actually members of middle- or upper-income families.[6] Furthermore, higher minimum wages tend to reduce available low-skill jobs. Grocery pricing and checkout by computer are examples of tasks now done by machine that were previously done by minimum-wage workers.

Their rhetoric notwithstanding, unions likewise have probably not affected the share of income going to workers—both because only one-fifth of the labor force is unionized, and because successful upward wage pressures are eventually matched by some tendency for employers to substitute capital for labor. The introduction of robotics into the automobile sector is an example of union labor displaced by capital. Higher wage demands by unions at a time when foreign competition was strong promoted such substitution of machines for workers. Furthermore, any independent effect that unions have on the distribution of income among individuals is probably at the expense of the *very* poor. This happens when high wage demands by unions reduce the number of jobs in unionized sectors and thereby put downward pressure on wages in low-skill,

6. See the studies cited by Ronald Ehrenberg and Robert S. Smith in *Modern Labor Economics: Analysis and Public Policy,* 2d ed. (Glenview, Ill.: Scott, Foresman, 1985), p. 78.

nonunionized sectors—into which workers who have lost their unionized jobs might move and compete for jobs with those already there.[7] So while high minimum wages or union rates may help some workers, economists have long recognized that they deprive others of employment simply because they prevent people with low-valued skills from offering to do jobs at low pay.

Over the period when the greatest gains against poverty were made (1929-1948), what role did government intervention—in the form of progressive income taxation (a tax system where tax rates as a percentage of income are higher for the rich than for the poor) and transfer payments—play in reducing income inequality? The high visibility of FDR's New Deal, of the creation of a Social Security system, and of the advent of various welfare programs might lead us to credit government intervention with the lion's share of reduced income inequality. But this does not appear to be the case. According to one extensive study of this question,[8] government redistribution of income at the very least augmented by 40 percent a salutary drop in the income concentration ratio being brought about by the other changes we noted above; at the very most, government doubled the drop in inequality which was occurring for other reasons. In short, government programs for income support and redistribution played a significant role, but other economic changes which we mentioned (such as higher levels and greater quality of education for workers) promoted equality at least as much as and probably more than explicit public tax and spending policy did.

In our review of the data on the incidence of poverty (as opposed to the overall distribution of income) between 1950 and 1979, we already suggested that government in-kind benefits further reduced poverty no matter how it was measured. In addition, economic growth itself is responsible for a good share of this improvement, because many people who were poor were pulled above the poverty line as the average standard of living for the population rose. In the period from 1967 to 1979, economic growth and government monetary benefits contributed about equally to the decline in poverty rates. (The 1980-1982 recession at least temporarily wiped out the earlier gains made against poverty, raising the percentage of families in poverty from a 1973 low of 11.1 percent to 15.0

---

7. See Albert Rees, *The Economics of Trade Unions*, 2d rev. ed. (Chicago: University of Chicago Press, 1977), pp. 89-93.

8. The study is that of Irving Kravis, cited by Barry W. Poulson in *Economic History of the United States* (New York: Macmillan, 1981), p. 645.

percent).[9] Those who favor market solutions like to emphasize the role that economic growth has played in reducing poverty, suggesting that we should rely less on government and more on economic growth for further gains against poverty. A fuller explanation of reduced poverty levels would require us to examine specific historical forces at work on the economy—the post–World War II boom, the Korean War, even the different emphases of two political parties and of various U.S. presidents and their greater or lesser commitments to poverty programs.

The fact that progress against poverty was made for a variety of reasons does not diminish our responsibility to deal with the problems that remain. What more ought we to do as a nation and as individuals to reduce both relative inequality (the concentration ratio) and absolute poverty (the percentage of the population living below the poverty line)? This is a very difficult question, both in moral and practical terms. But before we tackle it directly, we need to take a closer look at the relative positions of today's poor, at the movement of people into and out of poverty, and at the degree of their dependence on welfare. In this area, as in so many others, economic analysis leads to much more understanding than does popular rhetoric that demeans the poor.

WHO THEN ARE THE POOR AMONG US TODAY?

Despite the apparent statistical improvement in the distribution of income and the reduction of poverty (as we have defined it—in terms of a minimum dollar budget) to a mere 3-6 percent of the population by the late 1970s, certain statistics still shock many of us. While the median monetary income for U.S. families in 1983 was about $25,000,[10] nearly 17 percent of U.S. families had money incomes of less than $10,000 in that year. Furthermore, during 1979 the median income for a Mississippi family was less than three-fourths the national median. And in 1983 the median income for black families across the United States was only 56 percent of that of white families—*down* from 62 percent in 1975. Even if government transfers of various kinds alleviate physical hardships faced by the poorest members of the population, they don't do nearly so much

9. See Peter Gottschalk and Sheldon Danziger, "A Framework for Evaluating the Effects of Economic Growth and Transfers in Poverty," *American Economic Review* 75 (March 1985): 153-61.

10. For income data cited in this paragraph, see the U.S. Bureau of Census, *Statistical Abstract of the United States: 1985,* 105th ed. (Washington: Government Printing Office, 1984), pp. 446, 447, 450.

to reduce either the effects of "relative poverty" (reflecting the gap between living standards of the rich and the poor) or the often demoralizing impact of dependency on an institutional, outside "bread giver" rather than a home-based "breadwinner."

This leads us to an interesting question: What is the degree of dependency on welfare in the United States? A recent study done at the University of Michigan by Richard D. Coe produced several striking findings. It appears that, whereas approximately 10 percent of a representative sample of Americans were in households that received some welfare assistance during any given year between 1969 and 1978, fully 25 percent of the representative sample (one out of every four persons!) were in households that received welfare some time in the ten-year period. However, less than one-fifth of all those who were on welfare at one time or another during the ten-year period were long-term recipients (i.e., persons receiving assistance for eight to ten years out of the ten-year period studied). Nearly half were short-term recipients (persons receiving welfare for only one to two years), and their composition in terms of age, race, and sex was so close to that of the general population as to warrant a judgment that no single demographic group appears to be particularly immune from an occasional bad year, during which its members turn to welfare for some help. Furthermore, only about one in thirteen of those individuals receiving welfare at some time over the decade were "dependent" on it for a long time (i.e., receiving 50 percent or more of their income from welfare during eight to ten years of the decade studied). A disproportionate number of these were females and their young children.[11] In short, long-term dependency on welfare is the exception. The data suggest that, despite myths surrounding the welfare system, it is not in fact promoting an enervating financial dependency.

According to Coe's study, the poor of this country are by and large not a permanent caste of dependents who produce more dependents, nor are they people who simply won't work. In 1969, for instance, 57 percent of all the poor were in the labor force (either employed or actively looking for work). Of the rest, many were elderly or part of female-headed households with small children, and thus suffered from poverty for which employment was not a viable solution.

It is important to note that there are significant reasons for expecting that many people will pass through periods of poverty but will not spend their lifetimes in such a state. If, instead of calculating income distribu-

11. Coe, "Welfare Dependency: Fact or Myth?" *Challenge: The Magazine of Economic Affairs* 25 (Sept.-Oct. 1982): 43-49.

tion at one point in time, we were able to get data on *lifetime* incomes, these would prove to be much more equal than incomes earned in a single year. Why is this so? A young person attending high school or college may have low net earnings. But after he or she begins to work, net earnings will typically rise, peak as the person reaches his or her late forties or early fifties,[12] and then fall. Incomes in retirement years tend to be still lower. During their working lives, individuals will be likely to experience periods of unemployment and departures from the labor force, both of which temporarily lower their incomes. Consequently, among those counted as "the poor" in any single survey year, there will be disproportionately large numbers of the young, the old, the unemployed, and people temporarily out of the labor force.

The various income-maintenance programs now in place at state and federal levels are designed to assist people through a period of hardship. The study of welfare "dependency" reported above suggests that by and large the system usually does operate to cushion income during a short period of time. By implication, the study also points to our society's need to examine what more we can do to help the minority who are not able to escape poverty and welfare dependency.

WHERE DO WE GO FROM HERE?

If the public policies created to alleviate poverty made real gains up until 1979 (though undoubtedly not all the gains their supporters had hoped for), should we press for much more of the same—i.e., continue some mix of higher income transfers and subsidies for food, housing, education, and other things—and increase taxes in order to pay for them? There is no single right answer to this question. In recent years economists have examined, in much more detail than before, the hidden costs of taxes and transfers, especially their potential impact on incentives. These studies highlight one reason why we can expect that any further gains to be made in the battle against poverty will, in all likelihood, come at greater incremental cost.

WHAT ARE THE COSTS OF FURTHER INCOME REDISTRIBUTION?

The drawbacks of additional anti-poverty efforts are connected to the effect that raising taxes has on both taxpayers and benefit recipients. Consider first the low-income beneficiaries of transfer programs. The only way to provide substantial protection to families whose incomes

12. See Ehrenberg and Smith, *Modern Labor Economics*, p. 246.

temporarily dip to nearly zero while at the same time making sure that welfare is received by only a minority of the population is to rapidly reduce benefits (whether in-kind benefits or income transfers) as family earnings rise. This is a simple mathematical truism that can be illustrated by a few examples.

The median family income in the United States in 1979 was approximately $20,000. In that same year, according to federal determinations, a family of four was considered below the poverty line if they earned $7,000 or less. Suppose we believed our government should protect people against poverty to the extent of not permitting the income of a family of four to drop below $5,000 (a sort of guaranteed minimum "safety net"). Of course, we could do this by simply giving families a monetary payment equal to the difference between $5,000 and their actual incomes. Thus, a family would receive $5,000 if they earned no money that year, but only $1,000 if they earned $4,000. The trouble with such a system is that there would be no financial incentive to earn the majority of the $5,000, since benefits would make up any difference.

One proposed solution to the problem of severely reduced work incentives is an arrangement that guarantees a minimum untaxed income level for all families and a benefit cutback rate substantially less than 100 percent for every dollar earned above the minimum income. The guaranteed minimum income and benefit cutback rate can be combined at various levels so that the incentive to work is not squelched by a drastic reduction in benefits. One such combination is a guaranteed minimum of $5,000 and a benefit cutback rate of 50 percent, such that benefits are cut back by 50 cents for every dollar earned. Unfortunately, while it effectively addresses the problem of work incentives, this particular combination would increase the number of welfare recipients: people with earnings as high as $10,000 would receive some welfare benefits. For 1979, this would be the equivalent of just over 20 percent of the U.S. population (assuming the average family consisted of four persons).

On the other hand, if we wanted to make sure that no one earning more than $7,000 received welfare, then benefits would have to be reduced at the rate of seventy-one cents for every dollar earned. While this would lower the percentage of families receiving welfare to about 7 percent, such a high cutback rate for benefits would seriously hamper any incentive the poor might have to earn an income. One estimate of the actual cutback rate that applied to the average low-income family in the mid-1970s was sixty-five cents on the dollar earned, meaning that for many people it was much higher still.

Advocates of this form of assistance (called a negative income tax) want all welfare to be consolidated into a single direct-income transfer. They believe that this would not only allow the poor to make their own budget decisions but also reduce the disincentives that are now cumulative for families facing separate benefit cutback rates for Aid for Dependent Children, food stamps, housing subsidies, and so on. For instance, a family receiving several such benefits can actually lose twenty-five cents' worth of food stamps, forty-five cents in housing subsidy, and twenty-five cents in Aid for Dependent Children for every dollar earned. This implies a total cutback rate of approximately 95 percent, and in some cases it exceeds 100 percent.

Apart from attempts to remove bureaucratic waste and fraud or major shifts in government budgets, any attempt to increase the level of benefits to the poor implies that taxpayers will face higher average and marginal tax rates. Our federal income tax schedule consists of pyramiding tax brackets that tax from 11-50 percent of an individual's income. These are marginal tax rates, indicating the share of the last dollar earned that the taxpayer contributes in taxes. However, because exemptions and deductions make taxable income less than total income, the average rate of taxation of total income will be less than the marginal (i.e., bracket) rate. As marginal tax rates are raised to pay for additional benefits to the poor (or for any other budgetary increase), decisions by middle- and upper-income families about whether it's worth their while to work an extra hour might be adversely affected—with serious repercussions for the whole economy.

Higher marginal tax rates (which take the form of higher benefit cutoff rates for the poor) are a legitimate cause for worry because they generate disincentives. Although there may be all sorts of good purposes to which the additional tax revenues can be put, the higher rates can discourage productive effort. They can reduce the number of hours some people want to work; discourage others from getting the education necessary to gain access to higher-paying professions; reduce the general attractiveness of high-risk, high-responsibility occupations; invite earlier retirement; lower the incentive for more than one family member to work outside the home; increase the attractiveness of consumption over saving; and so forth. Just how sensitive people are to marginal tax rates is a subject that is still much studied and much debated. Concern over high tax rates has been the hallmark of supply-side economics. If the disincentives are large enough, a logical implication is that higher tax rates (to pay for welfare) could actually leave the poor worse off by reducing the gross national product. That is, the higher taxes could make the total economic pie smaller and thereby reduce the *dollar value* of the increased share going to the poor in welfare benefits.

Clearly, whether more can or should be done to redistribute income toward the poor is an extremely complex question. The relevant question is, "What would it cost to do so, relative to the benefits received by the poor?" One estimate is that a redistribution of only 1 percent of national income to the poorest fifth of the population would require a redistribution of another 1 percent to the nonpoor (due to the problems associated with setting acceptable benefit-reduction rates, which in turn means that some benefits would reach those with relatively good earnings), and would result in pushing up marginal tax rates by 10 percent.[13]

The economic question is, "How much would this increase in marginal tax rates reduce productivity by discouraging effort and altering resource allocations?" A related moral question is, "Are we justified in increasing efforts on behalf of the poor if doing so also redistributes monetary income among the middle classes?" To what extent is equity enhanced by taxing income away from a two-career, childless couple in order to assist a one-career family who choose to have one parent remain at home? To what extent is equity served by taxing away the income of a harried, middle-level manager to support a teacher for whom the enjoyment of children and greater time flexibility is sufficient to compensate for a more modest salary?

BESIDES FURTHER INCOME REDISTRIBUTION, WHAT OPTIONS EXIST?

While there is considerable movement into and out of poverty, we noted earlier that for certain subgroups of the population the incidence and duration of poverty are disproportionately high, as is the degree of their dependence on welfare. This is especially the case for racial minorities, and particularly so for black women with small children. In this country, blacks suffer the consequences of a long, ignoble history of racial discrimination that limits their access both to good education and to financially rewarding jobs. Even when overt discrimination in education decreases, inequalities in educational levels achieved can persist for a variety of reasons. A child of a poor black family who cannot rely on family resources to finance his or her education will often find it more difficult to get bank loans for college and face more family pressures to

13. Browning estimates that nearly all families would be paying marginal rates over 50 percent (see "How Much Equality Can We Afford?").

choose a paying job now over continued education and delayed financial reward. Furthermore, if the child is black and female, she may reasonably be discouraged from pursuing a college education because her expected market rewards for an extra year of schooling are less than those of a male child, black or white. The latter follows in part from the crowding of women into certain low-paying jobs—a result of both discrimination and social expectations regarding household sex roles.

To the extent that limited access to financial resources for education and training is one handicap faced by poor minorities, an obvious public policy remedy for long-term poverty among them is to provide need-based educational subsidies—both grants and low-interest loans—as well as income assistance during training. (Christians might see in this an echo of the Old Testament establishment of the Year of Jubilee, which proposed the redistribution of land—the existing capital—to break intergenerational cycles of poverty.) Because the concentration of poverty is higher among mothers of young children, any effort to assist them in acquiring marketable skills would have to take into account a complementary need for financially accessible and responsible child-care.

To some extent, discrimination in access to jobs and pay also contributes to the incidence of poverty among minorities. The provisions of the Civil Rights Act of 1964 were designed to require equality of treatment in hiring practices, pay, and other employment conditions. However, that act covers only employers in interstate commerce with at least twenty-five employees. Affirmative action plans—demonstrating how firms intend to remedy the underutilization of women and minorities—are a further policy tool against discrimination. Large firms doing business with the federal government are required to develop such plans. Although there is not unanimity on the issue, most economic studies suggest that some of the improvement in black/white earnings ratios since 1964 can be attributed to both the civil rights act of that year and the requirement of affirmative action plans from federal contractors. What more can be done will depend in part on the amount of resources devoted to enforcement, as well as on the possible extension of such protection to employees of firms doing business within a single state and/or firms having contracts with nonfederal governments.[14]

Earlier we noted that lower levels of unemployment since World War II have been one factor explaining a trend toward greater equality in income. It is also the case that lower unemployment levels prior to the late 1970s partially accounted for improvement in the incomes earned by

14. See Ehrenberg and Smith, *Modern Labor Economics*, pp. 412-20.

blacks relative to those earned by whites. Consequently, macroeconomic policies (i.e., federal tax and spending policies), the aim of which is to ensure high employment levels generally, are also an important anti-poverty tool. Improving the public subsidy of job training for nonwhites, as well as providing them with greater assistance in getting and holding jobs, could help combat unemployment and low pay, two principal causes of their poverty.

IMPLICATIONS

Our discussion of twentieth-century U.S. public policy toward the poor should give us a certain appreciation for the progress that was made while also sensitizing us to the difficulties of doing much more taxing to pay for higher benefits to the poor. Liberals may take a degree of legitimate pride in promoting welfare concerns, while conservatives (and others) deserve credit for calling our attention to some of the hidden costs of welfare and income redistribution, and to the possibility that the additional costs of doing much more income transferring will rise rapidly. Obviously, income redistribution in favor of the poor could be taken further without having extremely adverse effects on incentives if increased help for the poor were to come out of changes elsewhere in the federal budget, such as a reduction in military spending. Instead, the opposite has happened during the Reagan administration.

This does not mean that there is little Christians can contribute to the discussion of public policy toward the poor. Those who believe that the general direction of policy since World War II has been a reasonable response to society's obligation to protect the poor against undue hardship will want to restore welfare effectiveness to its pre-1979 level and prevent a diminishing of these efforts on behalf of social/military expenditures that are perhaps less worthy. This and tax relief for the working poor have been the focus of lobbying by such groups as Bread for the World and the Catholic bishops. Other Christians, persuaded by the logic of the market, may believe that by 1980 we had gone too far in the fight against poverty, citing lessened productivity and tax and welfare measures taken that may have unjustly deprived the well-off of the fruits of their efforts and the poor of their dignity. These Christians will have a special interest in various kinds of welfare reform and perhaps an equal obligation to realistically estimate the degree to which private charity could possibly supplant public transfers. Still other Christians—those sensitive to the radical critique of the market's failure to promote a sharing of abundance with certain minorities—will want to promote public measures to rectify unequal access to education (e.g., by heavily subsidizing minority students' fees) and to jobs with a future. They will call for vigorous enforcement of the provisions for equal pay and affirmative action now in place. Finally, to deal with unemployment-induced poverty, they may favor the pursuit of high employment levels while accepting the implied higher inflation rate (or lesser efficiency, which can result from across-the-board price controls). This last conflict of goals, and the trade-offs implied, will be the subject of Chapter Nine.

Christians cannot avoid the biblical injunctions to exercise concern for the poor—both through personal efforts and through collective measures. The question that remains for individual Christians to answer is "How?" We cannot be "let off the hook," despite some inevitable disagreement among those who try to account for poverty and propose solutions. The solutions may range from minimum reliance on government intervention to heavy reliance on government intervention, but no solution is without cost. Large-scale public measures can be undertaken at a certain cost to both freedom and efficiency, and at their worst may actually lead to greater equality at *lower* standards of living for everyone. Such measures also cannot be expected to distinguish between the "deserving poor" and those who are poor due to irresponsible choice.[15] On the other hand, small-scale private charities may avoid indiscriminate largesse, but overlook those "deserving poor" who follow a religion that the charity would not support or who are hidden by racial, social, and geographical distance from the aid-givers. Furthermore, certain personal disciplines such as striving to live more simply must be combined with direct aid to the poor if they are to both leave the heart less encumbered and effectively improve the conditions of poor people. Whether public policy, private charity, or individual life-styles are in question, we need to continually attend to the gaps that reappear between well-meaning intention and actual success in aiding the poor.

Questions for Further Consideration

1. The 1984-85 letter of U.S. Catholic bishops on the U.S. economy called for a moratorium on "blaming the victims" of poverty. How can we avoid this tempting error and at the same time devise policies that respect

15. The issue of deservedness is typically given much more attention in today's public debate than in the Scriptures. Biblical teaching does not portray the suffering of the poor as generally resulting from their own foolishness or immorality. It suggests they suffer because of many misfortunes, actual abuse, or neglect.

the important role incentives play in the choices people make that affect their incomes?

2. Does the Bible really teach that something more than personal charity is owed to the poor? If so, how do twentieth-century government social programs embody or undermine those obligations?

3. The quotation from Adam Smith at the opening of this chapter focuses on the right of poor persons to use their labor to support themselves. What questions does this raise about the ethics of minimum wage laws, which prevent some people with few skills from supplying their labor at a low wage?

4. As Marx well understood (see the quotation from him at the beginning of this chapter), workers in market economies suffer from the vagaries of the market. Does this suggest to you that labor markets should be eliminated, cushioned, or left alone?

5. Does your reading of the evidence presented in this chapter make you more or less pessimistic about public welfare policy than Thomas Malthus, who is quoted at the beginning of this chapter?

6. The Reagan administration's cuts in welfare coverage played a role in the recent rise in poverty rates. What position do you think Christians should take on this matter, and on the reform proposals that would reverse the trend toward higher taxation of the working poor?

CHAPTER FIVE

Poverty among Nations: Hope for Those Who Live at the Bitter Margin

I am poor because you are rich.

President Nyerere of Tanzania

People (and nations) are hungry because they are poor, and they are poor because they lack income-generating employment, or power over their own lives, or in some cases land and other essential inputs to assure the fulfillment of their essential food needs.

John Sewell et al., *The United States and World Development*

In effect, just as our [Western] societies would not have been able to find their political and moral equilibrium without dealing with the problems of the disadvantaged, so also the freedoms that make up the best of Western traditions will hardly be able to survive in a world where differences between rich and poor, between black, yellow, and white are not overcome.

Jean Monnet, "La Communauté éuropéenne et l'unité de l'Occident"

Many of us need to squarely face our politely suppressed judgment that nations are poor primarily because their people are lazy or their leaders ignorant. Others of us ought to examine more carefully our feelings that nations are poor only because they have been exploited by the rich. While we who live in the wealthy countries of the world—a minority of twenty-five percent—were born with gold spoons in our mouths, the majority of the world's people were born with lead spoons worth less than one-tenth of our own. Of these, about a third were endowed with spoons worth only three cents to our dollar. Why *are* we so rich and they so poor? And of what moral and pragmatic concern is it to us? To some extent these are very similar to the questions we addressed with respect to domestic poverty. In exploring that topic we recognized that there is some link between effort expended and income received within an economy, but this appears to be much less true of the international distribution of incomes. Fifty Indians live on the average annual income of a single American. This has everything to do with resource endowments (gold or lead spoons) and very little to do with how willing an Indian is to work hard relative to an American.

Economists usually prefer to analyze economic systems in terms of their ability to supply the "wants" of consumers, not their "needs." Yet in the case of extreme poverty, needs are prominent, because the incomes and the resources of very poor people do not permit them much choice among wants beyond survival or among the means to meet their survival needs for food, shelter, and energy. Furthermore, Christians are particularly instructed by scriptural teaching and by the powerful symbolism of eucharistic bread and wine to care about and respond to the needs of the hungry and destitute. Consequently, in this chapter we will go beyond a survey of aggregate economic indices for poor countries in order to consider how well the needs of the poorest are being met and what development strategies are especially suited to meeting their most urgent needs.

ECONOMIC GROWTH YESTERDAY AND TODAY— PROGRESS FOR SOME, STAGNATION FOR OTHERS

Poor tropical soils leeched by heavy rains, climates not conducive to great physical exertion, the absence of large amounts of energy resources—historical comparisons of nations suggest that these factors have played some role in keeping today's poor nations poor. Undoubtedly more important, however, is the fact that the scientific and technological revolution, which started in the now industrialized nations, met with greater initial barriers in non-European civilizations. These barriers may have included both the absence of this-worldly interest among peoples who traditionally have believed themselves subject to recurrent life cycles and the Eastern notion that the physical universe is an illusion.

Such a line of reasoning is admittedly speculative and may miss the point that, after all, success breeds success as well as the appropriate mental attitudes to foster it. Whatever influences explain the Industrial Revolution, the fact remains that some late eighteenth- and early nineteenth-century Europeans took an interest in applying science to practical problems of material life, and others were able to seize on the possibilities to thereby make a profit. Among them was a sufficiently large number who saved and re-invested in similarly productive ventures rather than using their new riches to adopt an aristocratic life-style. All this happened at a time when population pressures were mitigated by a high death rate. Thus savings did not have to be shared with innumerable relatives; they could be re-invested, with a noticeable impact on subsequent production and income levels. It is not clear whether the Christian view of life especially favored this endeavor (a thesis made famous by Max Weber) by endorsing a certain degree of material success as a sign of God's favor, or whether the obvious success of incipient capitalist merchants and manufacturers actually altered Christians' thinking about material life and the possibility of progress.

In any case, history records that, while for most of human existence poverty was the nearly universal circumstance of individuals living in societies, Europeans were the first group to gain real momentum by seizing opportunities to expand production and trade, to save, and thus to further expand production and trade. They thereby established a gap between their living standards and those of the rest of the world, a gap that has widened over time.

RECENT EVIDENCE OF GROWTH IN POOR NATIONS

In our own day, of course, the seed of the scientific-technological-industrial revolution has not failed to take root in those nations originally left behind by Europe's burst of cumulative economic growth. We will refer to the "late bloomers" variously as poor nations, less developed countries, and developing countries, and to the early starters as rich nations or developed countries. Because our own living standard is so high and less developed countries have so far to go in making substantial improvements in their own living standards, we often fail to see progress that occurs gradually. Many of us who see photographs and statistics about the very difficult living conditions for people in the world's poorer countries have the impression that the entire development enterprise may be an exercise in disappointment for them. Perhaps this is why we often make a gloomy assessment of the prospects faced by three-fourths of the world's population that is poor. But is this a fair assessment? For an answer, we need to look at the recent record.

Many of today's less developed countries were economically stagnant—experiencing virtually no growth in their per-capita output—until after World War II. The burst of growth they then experienced during the quarter century between 1950 and 1975 exceeded the most optimistic projections of economic specialists. On average, developing countries enjoyed a 3.4 percent annual per-capita growth rate in the Gross National Product—a pace much more rapid than they had previously experienced, and even more rapid than that which any economically advanced nation had known prior to 1950. This is truly good news that deserves to be noted, perhaps even celebrated. It suggests that the factors that may have militated against Asian, African, and Latin American participation in Europe's early spurt in economic growth will not be permanent barriers against their achievement of higher standards of living.

The good news is not unclouded, however, because high average growth rates for less developed countries taken together mask considerable diversity of experience among them. Oil-exporting nations as well as Brazil, Korea, and Taiwan (whose per-capita GNP increased by 2.5 to 3.6 times!) were unexpected "success stories" during the period from 1950 to 1975. But India, Egypt, and Ghana were disappointments. India, with over one-fifth of the population of the less developed countries, was undoubtedly the greatest disappointment: its annual per-capita growth rate was only 1.5 percent. Nevertheless, even this low rate of growth permitted the average standard of living to improve by nearly 50 percent in twenty-five years.[1]

DIFFICULTIES AND CONSIDERATIONS IN ACCURATELY GAUGING "PROGRESS"

IRRELEVANT GOALS RESULTING IN UNDUE PESSIMISM

One reference point which is frequently offered up for our concern is the increasing "gap" between poor and rich countries. Because the rates of economic growth for both rich and poor countries during the period from 1950 to 1975 were almost identical, the ratio of average incomes in the two groups remained nearly constant (as it has since 1975). Thus, the "relative gap" in incomes was neither lessened nor widened significantly. However, given the fact that per-capita incomes in rich countries are more than ten times those in poor countries, similar growth rates produced a widening gap in absolute dollars. While the ratio of average per-capita incomes in less developed countries relative to per-capita incomes in developed countries declined modestly from 14.9 to 13.9 percent (a slight lessening of the "relative income gap") between 1950 and 1975, the dollar difference in per-capita incomes between rich and poor nations (the "absolute income gap" with inflation netted out) actually *rose* from $2,218 to $4,863. If recent growth rates continued, only eight developing countries (those that, like Taiwan, are now better off and growing more rapidly than others) would be able to close the absolute income gap between themselves and developed countries in less than one hundred years—and only sixteen could do so in less than one thousand years. Indeed, the vast majority of less developed countries could *never* be

1. See David Morawetz, *Twenty-five Years of Economic Development: 1950 to 1975,* World Bank Type II Report Series (Baltimore: The Johns Hopkins University Press, 1977), chap. 2.

expected to close the gap, since their rates of growth are lower than those of developed countries.[2]

How important are these depressing comparative statistics? Most economists, both within and outside the developing world, believe that closing gaps is not a relevant developmental goal. It *is,* however, important that peoples in the less developed countries experience substantial improvements in their standards of living within each generation. After all, why should Taiwanese, who experienced more than a tripling of their standard of living between 1950 and 1975, be depressed at the thought that it may take another seventy-five years to close the absolute gap between their own living standard and that of developed countries? For that matter, why should Malawians, whose living standard doubled in twenty-five years, curse the future if they face approximately a two hundred-year wait for the gap to be closed? Significant economic gains measured against a historical benchmark for a given nation surely deserve to be applauded and enjoyed no matter what the state of the income gap between rich nations and poor nations.

MEASURING IMPROVEMENTS IN THE QUALITY OF LIFE

It has become increasingly clear that rapid growth rates of per-capita GNP are not the only appropriate developmental goal. At best, changes in real, per-capita GNP over time tell us on average what has happened to the ability of people to purchase items available in the marketplace. However, these growth rates may say very little about the changing ability of the average person to meet basic needs. Consequently, a special Physical Quality of Life Index (PQLI) has been developed, based on country-to-country data for life expectancy, infant mortality, and literacy.[3] Its values range from an average of forty-one for the less developed countries with the lowest incomes, to ninety-four for all developed countries taken together. According to this index, the gap between less developed countries and developed countries is being closed at an annual rate of two percent. Thus, whereas the potential for progress in terms of closing the absolute, per-capita GNP gap is indeed dismal, the prospects are bright—if current rates continue—for significantly closing the physical-quality-of-life gap within fifty years.

---

2. See Morawetz, *Twenty-five Years of Economic Development,* chap. 2.

3. For much of the data in this and the following section, see William Loehr and John P. Powelson, *The Economics of Development and Distribution* (New York: Harcourt Brace Jovanovich, 1981).

Even more remarkable is the success certain very low-income countries have had in bringing the physical quality of life to levels previously thought possible only if the growth rate of the GNP was high. In the late 1970s, for instance, Tanzania enjoyed a PQLI of fifty, nearly identical to that of Libya, even though Tanzania's per capita GNP was only one-thirtieth of that of Libya. Or consider Sri Lanka, with a PQLI of eighty-one compared to Venezuela's seventy-nine, but with only one-fifteenth of Venezuela's per-capita GNP. It is worth noting that Tanzania and Sri Lanka's peculiar success in directly improving their populations' quality of life was achieved in the context of largely socialist ideologies and institutions. These countries chose to abrogate the market in order to more directly attack poverty, rather than wait for national economic growth itself to eventually improve living standards. The fact that in the late 1970s Sri Lanka rejected much of the socialist formula it once embraced may indicate some of the previously hidden political and economic costs associated with its choice of a socialist alternative to markets. It must be noted, however, that direct attacks on the worst conditions of poverty do not require that markets be largely abandoned and socialism embraced. As will be noted later, several countries have had considerable success in attacking poverty and improving the quality of life, but have done so while maintaining largely market-oriented economies.

ASSESSING THE PLIGHT OF THE POOREST IN THE GROWTH PROCESS

A look at the PQLI nudges us in the direction of another critical dimension in the assessment of economic progress and prospects for poor countries. The startling progress made from 1950 to 1975 in the average GNP per capita actually tells us nothing about how equally the income gains were distributed within a particular population. But data on income distributions are scarce and often contradictory. For instance, Brazil has often been held up to the world as an example of nearly miraculous growth and simultaneously criticized by those who claim that poor Brazilians were left out or even lost ground. However, various data on income distribution do not all point in the same direction. While the overall inequality of income increased in Brazil between 1960 and 1970, the share of income going to the poorest fifth of the population actually increased (their income grew at a rate of more than twice the national average). On the other hand, in both the Philippines and Costa Rica, the improved overall equality of income was accompanied by a fall in the share of income going to the poorest fifth of their populations. If instead of concentrating on income shares we concentrate on changes in *absolute* income levels of the poorest fifth of the populations of less developed countries, we find that economic growth has generally not hurt them. In only four of fifteen Latin American and Asian countries did the real income (purchasing power) of the poorest fifth of the population *fall* during the 1960s. (Unfortunately, one of these countries was India, with a population greater than that of all fourteen of the other countries combined.)

Does sheer economic growth in terms of per-capita GNP typically occur at the expense of the poor? In terms of absolute income levels, data for rapidly growing countries suggest that the opposite has been true. A strong correlation exists between their per-capita growth rates and the improvement of the real income levels of their poor. The data from more slowly growing countries are somewhat mixed. In slow-growing Sri Lanka, for example, the real incomes of the poorest have improved, while in Colombia and Peru they have fallen.

If growth itself does not always insure some equitable sharing of improved living standards with the poorest members of a population, what are the chief factors explaining changes in income distributions? In an excellent summary of many studies on the subject, economists William Loehr and John P. Powelson single out four causal categories: (1) human capital, (2) population growth, (3) changes in the economy's structure (especially transformations from rural to urban) and accompanying population migrations, and (4) and public policy.[4] The interplay of these factors affects the distribution of income. As we noted in the last chapter on domestic poverty, workers' increased educational levels partially explained the improved equality of income in the United States. A similar correlation is true for economies generally. Significant increases in education and training expenditures produce a wider dispersion of human capital than exists for physical or financial capital, so greater equality of income is promoted. Various studies point directly to a correlation between levels of basic education in less developed countries and the share of income enjoyed by the poor. Population growth, on the other hand, militates against improved status of the poor. (In the next section of this chapter we will discuss the possibilities of slowing population growth.) The physical distribution of a population has varying effects. In less developed countries incomes are generally much more equally distributed in agricultural sectors than in urban sectors; thus an increase in

---

4. Loehr and Powelson, *The Economics of Development and Distribution*.

economy-wide inequality is sometimes largely the result of heavy migration toward urban areas.[5] This appears to be the case for India.[6]

Public policy may also—wittingly or unwittingly—affect income distributions. Some developing countries have combined progressive tax rates with increased public expenditures on services benefiting the majority who are poor rather than the minority who are rich. Despite this, in most countries the absolute number of dollars spent on benefits like education for each member of the small upper-class far exceeds the dollar amounts spent per person among the vast numbers of poor. Economic stabilization policies, designed to reduce inflation and counter balance-of-payments problems, have in a number of countries (such as Indonesia, Brazil, and possibly Chile) been found to hurt the very poorest members of the population. It is also known that policies which promote mechanization of agriculture, such as artificially low interest rates (which are held down either by direct subsidy or as a result of tariff and foreign-exchange policies), will work against income equality, since they discourage employment in the agricultural sector where most people live.[7]

Thus far we have struggled with the problem of measuring the success of the attempts by less developed countries to promote economic development. Because a rising GNP is sometimes a mixed blessing for the poorest members of a society, we will now look at a "basic needs" approach to improving the welfare of the poorest within the populations of less developed countries.

ADDRESSING BASIC NEEDS—A DEVELOPMENT STRATEGY FOCUSED ON THE POOR

The World Bank and other international agencies that have a mandate to promote economic development are increasingly focusing on a "basic needs" approach rather than offering blanket support for anything that would raise the GNP. This new approach does not deny the importance of continued striving for higher growth rates in per-capita GNP. However, it does recognize the possibility that the benefits of growth will not always be adequately shared with the poor (whose needs are crucial). The basic

5. For a discussion of migration, see Loehr and Powelson, *The Economics of Development and Distribution*, pp. 111-12.

6. Depending on what happens to the incomes of new migrants, it is theoretically possible for migration to have the opposite impact on overall income inequality for an economy. For instance, the postmigration incomes of migrants moving from rural to urban areas might be high enough to reduce the large income inequality of cities. If this happened, their flow to the cities would reduce income inequality in the country as a whole.

7. See Loehr and Powelson, *The Economics of Development and Distribution*, p. 143.

needs approach also focuses on probable causal links between improvements in the well-being of the poor and the subsequent overall economic success of a country. We now turn to an examination of these links and of policies consistent with a basic needs approach.

A basic needs approach to development explicitly calls for focusing on people's minimal needs for food, health care, clothing, shelter, energy, and transport, as well as their need for some nonmaterial benefits such as meaningful economic participation and a sense of worth. The aim is to narrow the focus to "needs" and thus to discover more efficient means to meet those needs than purely "trickle-down" sharing of overall economic growth with the poor. It turns out, for instance, that redirecting health-care expenditures from expensive curative measures to preventive care for the masses produces large savings in budgetary resources. Basic needs strategies produce complementarities that also ultimately save on budgetary resources. Better nutrition among the poor, for example, reduces their medical-care requirements. It is also true that some health improvements (e.g., the eradication of parasitic diseases) actually lower nutritional requirements. In addition, more widespread basic education tends to improve nutritional levels and reduce dependence on curative medical services. Of course, better educated and healthier workers are also more productive. Another important long-run benefit of a basic needs approach is that it works to reduce infant mortality, better educate mothers, and make birth-control measures available—and thus significantly reduces birth rates. Greater contributions toward output and slower population growth rates are the very things that can add significant momentum to economic growth.

Various countries successfully addressing the basic needs of their poorest citizens are doing so in the context of differing economic systems. Taiwan and Korea, for instance, are highly market-oriented economies, Sri Lanka is a "mixed economy," China has a centrally planned economy, and Yugoslavia has a decentralized planned economy. Although their choices about overall economic organization differ dramatically, these nations have in common a fairly equal distribution of land, and perhaps also share an emphasis on widespread development of human resources through improved education and health.

What strategies are best suited to an attack on absolute poverty—that is, what policy programs can best promote the satisfaction of basic needs? And what possible contributions can people living in rich nations make toward such efforts? The Overseas Development Council (a research organization that studies development, assesses U.S. development policy, and regularly recommends policy changes) has argued that several targets for developing countries should be vigorously pursued between 1980 and the year 2000: the doubling of food production and of per-capita incomes, and the meeting of some minimum goals with respect to increased life-expectancy and adult literacy, so that the PQLI gap between rich and poor countries could be cut in half.[8]

It is generally recognized that reaching these targets will require strong political willpower within developing countries themselves, since reallocating expenditures for public health, education, and nutrition in favor of the poor means at the very least a slower rate of growth in public resources benefiting the rich. The clash of interests is even more apparent when land redistribution or tax reform is employed to meet basic needs. While the real commitment to basic needs has to be made at the national level, many observers believe that rich nations and international agencies can bolster the resolve of developing countries by giving more generous aid to those countries making the most determined strides in this direction. Furthermore, the international commmunity can reinforce such progress by undertaking a number of steps to reform international trade and credit arrangements. Together these reforms are sometimes referred to as a New International Economic Order (NIEO).

GOALS OF A NEW INTERNATIONAL ECONOMIC ORDER

This New International Economic Order that developing countries have been calling for usually includes the following types of changes: (1) opening the markets of developed countries to more manufactured exports from less developed countries; (2) expanding negotiations to stabilize and improve prices of such commodity exports; (3) renegotiating the development debts of less developed countries; (4) increasing the levels of development aid and making some transfers of aid automatic; (5) devising measures to increase transfers of technology from developed nations to less developed countries; (6) raising the international monetary reserves of less developed countries as well as their share in decision-making within international bodies like the World Bank; and (7) adopting international codes of conduct for multinational corporations.[9] We will deal briefly with several of these proposed changes, giving special emphasis to the possibility that they will be of mutual benefit to both rich and poor nations.

8. See John W. Sewell et al., *The United States and World Development: Agenda 1980* (New York: Praeger, 1980), p. 103.
9. See Sewell et al., *The United States and World Development*, p. 8.

ENCOURAGING TRADE

International trade has long been recognized as an important vehicle for economic growth. England's gradual movement in the nineteenth century toward trade free of distorting tariff barriers can be largely attributed to the influence of Adam Smith, the "father of economics." Smith argued that exchanges taking place in ever-widening markets produce enormous benefits: consumers enjoy lower prices, and producers reap profits made possible by increased specialization. No nation has ever been completely committed to free trade, and relapses into protectionism are not uncommon in periods of economic stress. However, the industrialized (generally non-Communist) nations, which recognized that the horror of the Great Depression was made much worse by tariff wars, have since 1960 committed themselves to a series of reductions in trade barriers evidenced by the Dulles, Kennedy, and Tokyo rounds of international tariff negotiations since 1963.

Unfortunately, the particular trade interests of developing nations have not been given very much attention in recent trade negotiations. Their interests include an expanded generalized system of trade preferences, which now eliminates duties in industrialized countries on many imports coming from less developed countries, as well as the elimination of quantitative restrictions on many exports from those countries. Essentially what is being called for is a lessening of the protective restrictions against the exports of poor nations so that they might earn the foreign exchange necessary to finance their own development. Trade is built on the basis of *mutual* benefits, and it can hardly be denied that this dimension of an NIEO is one in which both rich and poor nations stand to gain. For both of them, international trade is a powerful promoter of economic growth, high employment, and stable prices.

ADJUSTING THE PRICES OF EXPORTS FROM LESS DEVELOPED COUNTRIES

Similarly, there are distinct possibilities for mutual benefits if certain agreements can be reached to stabilize the prices of commodities that dominate the exports of less developed countries. The industrialized users of these commodities can benefit from guarantees of access and from the lowering of inflation as a result of more stable import prices. Poor nations, which rely heavily on a few export commodities, can benefit by being able to depend on steadier export earnings, which are absolutely essential to financing their development efforts. Some realization of potential mutual gains underlies a commitment negotiated in 1980 by representatives of both rich and poor nations to finance buffer stocks (i.e., supplies of certain commodities that would be stockpiled during years of abundance and released to the world market during years of extreme production shortfalls). The details have yet to be worked out.[10]

Whether efforts should be made not only to stabilize the prices of commodity exports from less developed countries but also to raise these prices has been an area of major difference between less developed countries and industrialized countries, particularly the United States. The prospects for agreement here are not good because the benefits are not mutual. While less developed countries stand to gain from higher export prices, their customers in developed countries stand to lose. Furthermore, many fear that artificially raised prices would reduce international economic efficiency and actually harm the poorest of the less developed countries. For example, OPEC's unilateral decision to raise oil prices in the 1970s resulted in tremendous setbacks for those less developed countries that did not produce oil. They had to curtail important development efforts, particularly in agriculture, because increased agricultural output depended on more widespread use of fertilizer, an oil derivative that became prohibitively expensive. These countries also accumulated enormous debts in purchasing badly needed imports.

FINANCING RELIEF IN FOREIGN-EXCHANGE CRISES

Some progress has been made by the International Monetary Fund in providing increased foreign-exchange financing for developing countries that are experiencing temporary balance-of-payments problems. On the other hand, the generally perceived need to provide the poorest countries with debt relief, for example, by readjusting interest rates and payment periods on loans has not been fully satisfied by international lending institutions and lender countries.

BOLSTERING AID FOR DEVELOPMENT

It must be noted that the aid effort by the United States has been dismal. Whereas most industrialized Western European countries raised the proportion of their GNP devoted to economic development assistance between 1970 and 1980, the United States allowed theirs to fall. By 1980 the United States ranked fifteenth out of seventeen most-developed nations (including some developed countries outside of Europe); its contribution

10. See Loehr and Powelson, *The Economics of Development and Distribution*, p. 298; Sewell et al., *The United States and World Development*, p. 16.

of economic aid to less developed countries equaled less than one-fifth of one percent of its GNP, while Norway and Sweden gave nearly one percent of their GNPs. In real purchasing power (with inflation netted out), the official development assistance of the United States actually fell from $2.9 billion in 1961 to $2.2 billion in 1978.[11]

Higher levels of official aid for development do not constitute the single most important factor in helping less developed countries escape from poverty. Nevertheless, aid is very important. Some of the poorest nations must rely on aid for eighty percent of the foreign exchange they need to bridge the gap between their precarious export revenues and the high import costs for food, machinery, and other items crucial to their development effort. Less developed countries in the middle bracket can depend more heavily on private loans and direct foreign investment to bridge the gap because their greater output and higher incomes make them better credit risks, but aid is still important to them. Despite occasional stories of aid funds having been misdirected into the pockets of corrupt leaders or local administrators, aid (especially when it is channeled through international agencies like the World Bank) serves as an important catalyst for economic development and a buffer against disaster in countries still highly vulnerable to the vicissitudes of weather, trade, and war. It complements (though it cannot substitute for) stable and well-managed governments, improved local rates of saving, and increased entrepreneurial energies devoted to raising productivity in all sectors of the economies of less developed countries.

PROVIDING FOR INCREASED SHARING OF TECHNOLOGY

In the realm of technology transfer, the United States has also dragged its feet on proposals to devote funds to improving the capacity of less developed countries to acquire and utilize technology. As far as energy policy is concerned, the United States—while not overly enchanted with adopting a substantial domestic conservation program—has strongly encouraged efforts by the World Bank and others to promote the exploration of energy resources and alternative energy development in less developed countries.

DIRECTLY ADDRESSING FOOD NEEDS

The United States has taken significant steps in the realm of food security by emphasizing aid for agricultural development in food-short

11. See Sewell et al., *The United States and World Development*, p. 233.

regions and by participating in negotiations to establish an international system of food reserves. We will say more about the crucial importance of increased food production shortly.

RICH AND POOR NATIONS—THEIR COMMON STAKE IN WORLD DEVELOPMENT

Beyond the specific NIEO proposals thus far discussed, a number of major challenges remain for the world's economies to confront. These further highlight some opportunities for mutual cooperation that are not yet fully exploited.

EXPANDING TRADE

Consider the key role that increased manufactured exports play in economic growth prospects, especially for less developed countries in the middle-to-high income bracket. Their export earnings help them pay for imports of both agricultural goods and high technology products coming from developed countries. And trade with less developed countries is increasingly crucial to the economic health of industrialized nations. By 1980, less developed countries accounted for 28 percent of the export sales of industrial countries (up from 23 percent in 1973). Yet Americans are especially prone to underestimating the important role that trade with less developed countries plays in their own economic well-being, despite the fact that by 1980, about 38 percent of total U.S. exports were purchased by developing countries (up from 33 percent in 1965).[12] These exports support large numbers of American jobs (estimated at half a million for exports going to less developed countries without OPEC affiliations). Since the early 1970s, these countries have represented the fastest-growing market for U.S. exports. Less developed countries as outlets for exports (as well as sources of imports) are also increasingly important to Western Europe and Japan. Given the strength of these commercial ties, it is a puzzle why industrialized nations have not seen fit in recent years to deal aggressively with the trade problems faced by less developed countries wishing to export more to industrialized nations. These problems include significant quota barriers against the very goods that less developed countries are most capable of producing competitively—for example, textiles, clothing, shoes, and TV sets.

12. See the World Bank's *World Development Report, 1983* (New York: Oxford University Press, 1983), p. 14; and the U.S. Bureau of the Census's *Statistical Abstract of the United States: 1981,* 102d ed. (Washington: U.S. Government Printing Office, 1981), p. 806.

Can industrialized nations long afford to forget that buying and selling is a two-way street, that less developed countries cannot continue to buy from industrialized nations at increasing rates if they cannot also sell their own exports? Can rich nations afford inflation that goes unchecked when imports are not allowed to compete vigorously with their own high-priced domestic output? (A recent survey found imports from less developed countries to cost 16.3 percent less than comparable U.S. products.)[13] In a new era of relative economic stagnation, can rich nations afford to pass up opportunities for trade expansion that stimulate investment and promote efficiency? For that matter, can they afford to overlook the potential for productive employment and income generation in population-rich less developed countries when population growth at home can no longer serve rich countries as a stimulus to demand and a means to increased production? Increasingly and inevitably, the economic success of developing countries is linked to that of industrialized nations. A renewal of economic growth and a higher standard of living for Americans, Europeans, and Japanese will depend in part on their ability to trade with less economically developed partners—trade that will likewise benefit these partners.

INCREASING FOOD PRODUCTION

Even the critical area of food production is susceptible to various interpretations in terms of mutual benefits to be derived by rich and poor nations if the production of less developed countries can be increased. The recent record of food production by less developed countries is dismal. In the entire decade of the sixties they increased per-capita production by only 8 percent (although total food output rose by 75 percent). In the seventies, per-capita increases were negligible. Since most of the world's population growth until the end of the twentieth century will take place in less developed countries, the only way their food needs can be met is either by vast improvements in their own food production capability or by food imports. Heaping enormous demands for food products on the economies of developed countries would vastly increase domestic food prices, so it is in the interest of these countries to assist less developed countries in increasing their own food production. Many experts believe that significant steps to increase the availability of land, credit, extension services, other agricultural inputs, and marketing channels to small farmers (as well as adjustments in pricing policies) in less developed countries could produce the incentives and means necessary

13. See Sewell et al., *The United States and World Development*, p. 29.

for greatly increased food output. This cannot be accomplished without an increase in aid resources devoted to such efforts. However, contrary to some all-too-common expressions of hopelessness, an estimate by the World Food Council suggests that actual increases in aid resources now being devoted to increasing food production in less developed countries may be nearly sufficient to meet a U.N. goal for food-deficient countries to increase their food output by 4 percent a year.[14] Of course, long-term goals of increased food production must in the short run be complemented by food relief for especially vulnerable groups in the poorest countries.

EMPLOYING MORE PEOPLE

The mutual interest that both poor and rich countries have in addressing population and employment problems deserves to be briefly explored here. Although developed countries experienced high unemployment rates in the early 1980s, their long-term prospects are for lower unemployment rates and a declining share of workers in the population. Poor countries face the opposite prospects. True, there are signs that less developed countries are succeeding in reducing their birth rates. A lower infant mortality rate is reducing the desirability of the many births once required to insure survival of a few offspring, and a greater access to birth-control methods is making smaller families possible. Nevertheless, for a long time to come the numbers of people entering the ranks of employable adults in less developed countries will continue its rapid rise. The acute problem this poses for generating jobs is mind-boggling. Estimates of the share of labor forces that are currently either unemployed or employed at life-threateningly low levels of productivity and income in less developed countries range between 40 and 45 percent—the equivalent of some 300 million workers.[15] What hope is there for these people to find jobs when the labor force in less developed countries (outside China) is expected to grow by another 500 million in the near future?

Even with the rapid industrialization of less developed countries, there is little likelihood that large numbers of workers could be absorbed into the industrial sector. Even extremely optimistic projections that less developed countries will gain an increased share of the world's industrial production indicate that such industrial expansion will provide jobs for

14. See Sewell et al., *The United States and World Development*, p. 62.
15. See Sewell et al., *The United States and World Development*, p. 82.

less than half the anticipated numbers of new entrants into the labor force in those countries. Consequently, if new entrants and currently under-employed and unemployed workers are to find adequate employment, the majority of new jobs will have to be found in the agricultural sector. Creation of these jobs is intimately linked to the basic needs approach to development. After all, remunerative jobs among the rural poor are the chief vehicle by which their needs will eventually be met.

Given the current labor prospects of developed and less developed countries, a mutually beneficial arrangement is obvious. The potential exists for Western industrialized countries to enjoy a return to economic growth by some combination of three factors: (1) an influx of foreign labor to reduce possible domestic labor shortages; (2) an increase in exports of technological products in exchange for more efficiently produced, labor-intensive imports from less developed countries; and (3) increased capital investment in less developed countries to take advantage of abundant labor supplies there. Clearly, all these measures have the potential of simultaneously providing more jobs and a better life for those of less developed countries as well.

TAXING "THE COMMONS"

Another possibility for change that would be mutually beneficial to both rich and poor countries is an international agreement to oversee and tax resources that are still the common property of all peoples, like the sea and space, sometimes referred to as "the global commons." It has long been recognized that user taxes can be applied to prevent the environment from being overused just as North American prairies were once over-grazed. Such taxes could be collected by an international agency and channeled into development assistance loans and grants, thereby preserving our common heritage while also promoting the welfare of those who are latecomers in natural resource development and utilization for economic growth. Barbara Ward, the well-known British economist, has powerfully argued that the world has reached a stage paralleling that of European nations in the 1840s. In that period in the nineteenth century, after weathering several violent revolutions, European nations extended the vote to the poor and eventually adopted vast social reforms—including laws regarding workplace conditions and welfare/workfare for the poor that were designed to bring the poor into the economic mainstream. Now, in the 1980s, we face a similar crossroads: either we "extend the franchise" to the world's poor and adopt planetary tax systems that could produce revenues to finance the improved productivity and well-being of poor nations, or we could see a breakdown in world order as a result of violent outbreaks between poor and rich nations.[16]

SUMMARIZING THE CHALLENGES

We have described the fundamental causes of poverty among nations. The second quotation opening this chapter effectively highlighted the chief links: hunger results from poverty, and poverty results from the lack of productive employment that can generate adequate income to meet life-sustaining needs. History should make us more surprised to find some nations now rich than to find many still poor. However, significant post–World War II economic progress and demographic transitions in developing countries give us good reasons to hope that a majority of the world's population may escape from life at the bitter margin within two generations.

However, this will surely not happen without concerted worldwide efforts. Significant political and institutional changes will have to be effected in developing countries before the poor within their borders can expect better fare. Basic needs strategies, land reform, and accelerated agricultural development are likely to be part of the answer to their plight. Rich nations will also have to play a supportive role if progress in developing countries is to be perceptible within a generation. Most experts would argue that the role of rich nations ought to include significantly more aid and better leadership in reforming international financial institutions. This would allow both for greater participation by less developed countries and for the creation of effective measures to meet their recurring financial needs.

We also suggested that there are vast realms of mutually advantageous endeavors that ought to be seized upon by rich and poor nations cooperating together. Trade is an expression of interdependence, and the benefits created by trade have therefore been called the fundamental "virtuous circle." Some critics will claim that emphasizing *mutual* benefits falsely implies that there is no moral dimension to international poverty. They argue that if the rich countries help less developed countries, they will simply be helping themselves by creating better customers. This criticism is not entirely unfounded. True, steps taken to help those less developed countries that are most economically distressed can be taken only on the basis of charity, because whatever payoff rich nations may reap from

16. See Mahbub Ul Haq, *The Poverty Curtain: Choices for the Third World* (New York: Columbia University Press, 1976), pp. xiii-xiv.

such investment will be far off. On the other hand, the prospects are good for rich countries to reap dividends from facilitating and financially assisting the development efforts of less developed countries in the middle-income and higher-income brackets. (Qualitatively, they are not unlike those benefits anticipated from both the Marshall Plan for European postwar reconstruction and the Dulles, Kennedy, and Tokyo rounds of international tariff negotiations since 1963.) For example, in a recent report by the University of Pennsylvania to a United Nations agency, it was estimated that a 3 percent increase in the growth rate of non-OPEC developing countries could lead to an annual 1 percent increase in the growth rates of developed countries.

Other critics of rich nation–poor nation cooperation question whether international intercourse as we know it has ever been anything other than an exploitative one-way street. But we believe there is strong evidence that trade is playing an important role in the marked success of some relatively high-income developing countries. It is true that highly monopolized forms of trade have existed which have left some less developed countries without the leverage necessary to gain a significant share of the mutual benefits generated. This kind of imbalance is undesirable, but steps can be taken to rectify it. We favor measures that would increase the share of trade benefits going to less developed countries by enhancing competition for their exports. Further reductions in the trade barriers of industrialized nations—especially quantitative ones—would help do just that.

IMPLICATIONS FOR CHRISTIANS

Christians have traditionally been at the forefront of historical movements on behalf of the rights and welfare of poor people within their own national borders. Today, too, they can play a significant role in marshaling the will and the resources to attack international poverty. In this chapter we have stressed international cooperative measures that could facilitate economic development generally and also insure that the poorest people within less developed countries would be beneficiaries of development. The Bible repeatedly shows God expressing concern for the rights and well-being of the poor. God's example inspires and encourages many Christians to embrace "basic needs" as the best development strategy—precisely because it focuses directly on the poor. They lend their support to such organizations as Bread for the World, which lobbies the U.S. government to increase its overseas development aid and to use its influence in international forums to direct aid efforts toward meeting basic needs. Other Christians have responded to God's commands to look out for the poor primarily by supporting direct, private (especially church-sponsored) relief projects, some of which also emphasize development.

How should we compare these two approaches? The relative financial importance of government aid to total development assistance is very great. For example, U.S. government development assistance to less developed countries in 1978 equaled 4.8 billion dollars, compared to only 0.9 billion dollars from private voluntary sources.[17] (It is disturbing to note that both government and private assistance, as percentages of the U.S. GNP, decreased during the decade of the 1970s, whereas in most other aid-donor countries, assistance of both kinds grew as a share of the GNP.) Of course, simply because the dollar value of voluntary aid is less than one-fifth that of government aid does not necessarily mean that voluntary aid is qualitatively less significant to the development effort. Most evaluations of private voluntary aid suggest, instead, that development projects undertaken by churches and other voluntary agencies are valuable models and catalysts for changes that will make life better for the poorest people within less developed countries.

It is our belief that neither private charity nor government aid by itself sufficiently witnesses to God's love and reflects his call for justice to the poor. These two forms of support should be complementary. We have noted that some developing countries already enjoy a self-sustaining momentum of growth that makes them attractive partners for developed countries in mutually advantageous endeavors that will strengthen the economies of both. However, many very poor nations will for the foreseeable future require the kind of help that does not pay off in material returns for the giver. Christians ought to be alert to this distinction and be at the forefront of renewed efforts to bolster the U.S. commitment to highly concessionary aid for development in the poorest of the less developed countries; and they should support international negotiations which facilitate continued development successes in those less developed countries that are more advanced.

Christians ought to be in a position to call Americans to task for an inexcusable reduction of their private and public aid efforts relative to their own increased standard of living during the 1970s. Christians might well reflect on the strange paradox of the tremendously rapid growth of Christianity in the Third World (especially in Africa) at a time when the

---

17. See Sewell et al., *The United States and World Development*, p. 225.

bonds of brotherhood/sisterhood expressed in the form of material assistance are weakening. Christians might also find biblical support for the creation of international arrangements to tax the use of "the global commons" to provide additional revenue for development assistance. Furthermore, economically well-informed and thoughtful Christians ought to be able to critique the disproportionate emphasis that nations have put on military expenditure compared with development assistance. In 1980, for instance, military expenditure by NATO nations was approximately ten times the amount of the economic development aid from all non-Communist industrial nations. The scandal is evident even among less developed countries, twenty-two of whom spent in excess of 5 percent of their own GNPs for military purposes during 1980.[18]

In sum, Christians ought to be in a position to remind each other and the world that extreme poverty is a curse and that we must apply all available means to eliminate it. We cannot allow ourselves to mistake laziness and general ineptitude as the chief causes of persistent poverty, nor wisdom and moral rectitude as the primary explanations for our own riches. The stability of the world in the long run depends on our success at this task. Even more urgently, the love of God and our neighbor demands that we make an all-out effort.

Questions for Further Consideration

1. Many (perhaps most) Americans regard the prospects for improved living standards in poor nations as very dim. Why? Is it a matter of inadequate information on past trends, misrepresentation by the media of current conditions, a desire to avoid appeals for help (because we want to feel good about keeping income we think we have justly earned), or something else?

2. Is it generally true, as President Nyerere says in the quotation that opens this chapter, that one nation is poor because another nation has done better at their expense? If so, economic aid should rightly be called "reparations." If, on the other hand, nations are poor because their people "lack income-generating employment" (see the full quotation from Sewell at the beginning of this chapter), then what roles should trade and aid play in the relationship between rich and poor nations?

3. What does evidence of the plight of the poorest people within poor nations suggest about the proper focus of development assistance, and

---

18. See *U.S. Foreign Policy and the Third World: Agenda 1983*, ed. John P. Lewis and Valerina Kallab (New York: Praeger, 1983), pp. 273-74.

about the degree to which economic growth alone or a "basic needs" focus is required to improve their lot?

4. What should be the balance between private voluntary and governmental aid efforts? What should Christians think and do about the dwindling relative aid burden borne by the United States, and about the current yoking of a large portion of U.S. aid to strategic interests rather than to demonstrated need.

CHAPTER SIX

Protecting Air and Water Resources

Civilization imperils the creation. . . . The picture of humanity's devastating impact on the creation of God is very grim. . . . The earth, air, water, and fire which sustain the life of humanity and all creation are in serious jeopardy.

Wes Granberg-Michaelson
A Worldly Spirituality: The Call to Redeem the Earth

Stunned by the putrefaction of Lake Erie. . . , many Americans have transformed their conception of the natural environment from a dumping ground to an object of religious devotion. The reaction to previous profligacy has been a conversion to fanatical devotion to environmental protection.

G. C. Bjork, *Life, Liberty, and Property*

Much well-meaning environmental legislation has been a case of "triumph of the right might over the wrong right."

Three Worlds of Gulliver (film)

At least since the 1960s, most educated populations have become aware of environmental degradation and increasingly concerned about acting in ways that do less harm to the air, water, and land resources which they have inherited and will pass on to later generations. We feel more personally responsible for what happens to these resources. We remember hearing our parents directing us to clean up around a vacation campsite: "We must leave it in a better condition than we found it." In the late twentieth century, this seems to be an appropriate motto for our use of environmental resources generally.

The more difficult problem is knowing how to translate our personal concern for the environment into effective steps to restore and protect it. Many environmental groups propose stringent regulatory limits on resource use. They endorse court action against producers whose wastes have damaged wildlife, endangered human life, and/or created eyesores. They also urge consumers to buy and use goods whose production and waste disposal make fewer demands on the environment. This latter call to "responsible consumption" is appealing because it focuses clearly on individual behavior—something over which we each have more direct control than we do over legal, legislative, and regulatory measures.

Nevertheless, the call to "responsible consumption" can also be very confusing. After all, how do we know which products are putting the greatest demands on our environment? Which goods are produced in ways that generate unacceptable levels of heat, chemicals, and other waste? Or which manufacturers of a given product use processes that especially damage air, water, and land resources? Which items come in packaging whose disposal poses serious problems, and for which recycling is least efficient? Of course, various organizations are ready to provide interested persons with some lists of products to avoid buying because they rank high on the list of environmental enemies. As concerned people play the role of watchdog, they carry an increased moral burden even when grocery shopping. Responsible consumers often feel inadequate to the task. They must first acquire information about these environmental matters, then make complex choices requiring them to balance environmental concerns against those of nutrition, preparation and disposal time, and budgetary limits.

In this chapter we will employ economic analysis of air and water pollution to suggest that alternatives to the above dilemma exist. That is, we will see how most pollution may be better understood as a problem of aggregates rather than as a result of immoral personal choices. The best solutions will be seen to involve collective action to maintain air and water purity, but action that sends appropriate signals back to individual consumers and manufacturers about their use of air and water resources. These solutions will enable a consumer to use *prices* as a guide to the relative degrees of environmental burden imposed by different products. And the same signals will induce individual firms to produce in ways that simultaneously minimize *all* costs, including those now shifted to other users of the same air and water resources. This offers the prospect of our enjoying cleaner air and water at lower costs than we may now be paying for their protection and cleanup.

We will see that economic analysis of pollution does not eliminate moral choices but rather repositions the moral choices at the level at which decisions are made about our *aggregate* use of air and water resources. Caring about the environment then becomes less a matter of agonizing consumption decisions and more one of endorsing and voting for effective, financially acceptable approaches to pollution control. These approaches are appropriately decided upon at the aggregate level, but the means employed must have clear impacts on incentives affecting individual actions—whether I buy colored or plain toilet paper, for instance, and whether a firm treats wastes or alters production processes to reduce waste disposal into the air or water.

MARKET FAILURE AND LEGAL REMEDIES—A
MISTAKEN VIEW OF POLLUTION AND ITS CONTROL

The market system is often criticized by those who are concerned about environmental degradation. These critics seem to assume that dirty water and air must be the inevitable by-products of capitalism, a system in which self-interest and profit serve as key motivating forces. After all, what could we expect from such a narrow focus except the failure of producers to exercise any moral restraint in their use of our precious common heritage of lakes, rivers, seas, air, and sky? This kind of criticism would have us believe that while the market system has provided us with great material abundance, it has failed us in its handling of the environment. Few of us stop to consider that some waste is an inevitable by-product of production, whether it takes place in a market system or a socialist economy. The U.S.S.R. and China, for instance, have faced extreme pollution problems, even though ostensibly their production is not motivated by profit.

Given its limited vision, our society has chosen to treat the social ill of pollution by placing regulatory limits on the behavior of producers. The legislation and implementation of clean air and water acts in the United States have taken the form of requiring all producers to decrease (by certain percentages) the output of industrial and municipal pollutants into the air and water. So what we have experienced is a rule-based approach to environmental cleanup and protection. In order to set technically attainable limits for emissions into the air or water (termed "effluents" in the case of disposal into water), regulators determine what is the "best adequately demonstrated control technology." Violators of these limits are subject to fines and other penalties. In some cases, such as municipal sewage treatment, penalties for failure to comply are combined with subsidies to assist with the costs of required pollution abatement.

A rule-based approach toward environmental cleanup and protection is what most naturally follows from the picture of pollution as a sleazy crime against all of us. The crime is thought to result from some businesses giving little attention to their social obligations whenever these conflict with their earning the highest profit, while socially responsible firms, who willingly bear abatement costs, lose out in the competition. So, if pollution results from the failure of markets to respect our legitimate concerns for the quality of our environment, we find it quite reasonable to address that problem with a regulatory apparatus which directly constrains producers in their use of air or water for waste disposal.

Unfortunately, moral admonitions not to pollute are notoriously ineffectual. Furthermore, achieving standards set by law has proved to be very expensive and consequently subject to widespread avoidance, delays, and even reversals.

There is a different way of looking at the pollution problem that leads to a very different prescribed cure—namely, one pioneered by economists. We will examine the economic analysis of pollution in considerable detail, comparing it with the common view of pollution and environmental protection just outlined. The predominant economic view of pollution is that it results not from market *failure* but from the *absence* of markets in air and water resources. Consequently, the favored economic policy prescription for controlling pollution is to introduce market-like incentives, or to actually create markets in air and water where they do not now exist. But exactly why is this approach recommended, and how would it work? We will see that the "incentive approach" takes adequate account of self-interest as a motive for much private behavior and of the spillover effects that such behavior has on public welfare. We will learn why this approach offers the prospect of continued—and possibly greater—environmental protection at less expense. Finally, we will learn why Christian stewards must be concerned about real motives, effective controls, and reduced expense.

AIR AND WATER AS COMMON PROPERTIES

Very often, air and water resources are not owned by any private party but are shared by the whole community. They are the common property of all. In many times and places clean air and water have existed in such abundant quantities that their use by any one person or business has not diminished their quality or availability to other persons. However, the crowding of people and production into small areas results in a different situation in which one person's use of the air for burning trash or heating a home with a wood stove may reduce the availability of healthy air to his or her neighbors. Similarly, one firm's using a stream for water to cool some part of its production process may begin to pose problems for human and animal use of that water only when several other producers are using the same body of water.

When resources like air or water are so abundant that use by one does not diminish their availability to another, we may say that they are truly "free goods." On the other hand, once crowding creates a situation in which additional use—whether by individuals or businesses or towns—leaves less available to others, then air and water are no longer "free."

The difficulty is that any single user will be inclined to treat the air and water as free resources, using them with abandon, since the costs of diminished availability will be borne by others and not charged to that user. Furthermore, there is no strong incentive inducing that user to limit and/or modify his or her use of air and water, even if he or she becomes concerned about air and water contamination caused by the multiple users. Why? Because reduced use of air and water resources by one person among many may require considerable individual effort and expense while not appreciably affecting the quality of those resources.

Thus "pollution" of water and air resources occurs when, as a result of congestion, natural air and water systems are unable to adequately dilute and cleanse the household and commercial wastes dumped into them. Waste disposal by itself is not properly called pollution until it occurs in ways and amounts that do damage to other users of the air and water. Pollution is, therefore, primarily a problem of aggregates rather than of isolated individual misbehavior. (Of course, it's possible for even a single user to cause pollution by dumping large quantities of waste into a very limited resource, such as a small body of water.)

We are all familiar with the dilemma of congestion and the impotence of "socially responsible" personal choices to affect the outcome. Consider the crowd at a popular public performance. A few individuals can get a better view by standing up, but if many others take their cue and also stand, no one is able to see better than when all were seated (except, perhaps, very tall people). A public-spirited person in such a setting may decide to remain seated. Unfortunately, she or he will be the only one to suffer and will not have done very much—if anything—to help others gain a better view of the performance. Similar problems arise in rush-hour crowding of streets, seasonal crowding of public beaches, and even overfishing of public lakes and streams. Any single person does little to create a problem that results from many people behaving as if available lines of sight, city streets, state beaches, and trout in streams were all unlimited resources. It is difficult to see why any one person would feel strongly led to stay seated amid a standing audience, drive at an inconvenient time, stay away from the beach during the best sunning hours, or stop fishing after one catch, knowing that none of these sacrificial choices would alleviate the problem. Even the good feelings experienced by someone making these sacrificial choices are probably diminished by the small difference his or her restraint makes to the outcome. (It is true that in some limited cases, concerned resource users banding together can enhance the value of their own conscientious example by employing moral persuasion to influence the behavior of the general public.)

There are two principal ways of dealing with the problems of overuse of public resources, whether they be public waters, streets, beaches, or air: to make rules or create disincentives. Rules can be devised with appropriate procedures for detecting and penalizing violators. They may be strongly held and widely practiced informal rules for public behavior, such as the implicit rule of queuing up in England, where violators face public disapproval. Or they may be actual laws whose penalties include fines and imprisonment. We are familiar with the legal rule-making approach in many of the cases mentioned above. Traffic congestion is sometimes partially controlled by reassigning lanes from inbound city traffic during the morning rush hour to outbound traffic during the evening rush hour. Permission to fish or hunt is often regulated by season, location, and the limit that can be caught or bagged. Householders are also familiar with rules that establish "burn" and "no-burn" days for leaves and other refuse.

Much less familiar to us than rules and regulations is an approach that relies on creating new disincentives (or incentives) to induce changes in individual behavior that will reduce congestion and overuse of common resources. In the private market economy, congestion-like problems are reduced by price responses to changes in the relative scarcity of things. For instance, we are accustomed to finding prices higher during peak seasons—motel rates in Florida, for example, are higher in winter and early spring. Of course, when the price differential is great enough, some people will decide to travel or pursue recreational activities during the off-season. This has the simultaneous effect of reducing congestion in facility use during peak seasons and of improving earnings in recreational businesses during the off-season.

APPLYING AN INCENTIVE SYSTEM USING CHARGES
FOR AIR AND WATER USE

For over two decades economists have been suggesting that market-like disincentives and incentives be used in the sphere of environmental protection for air and water as well as in the management of other public resources subject to congestion problems. For instance, it would be relatively easy to mimic the private sector by adjusting bridge and road tolls to discourage their heavy peak-time use and to encourage reliance on less congestion-aggravating public transport. Economists have advocated a similar approach to protecting air and water quality.

Typically, whether as private households or as businesses, we have been charged little or nothing for our use of the water and air that belong to the community at large. We have faced no explicit disincentives that would regulate either our total use of air and water for disposal of waste, or the timing of such use. Consequently, while we have vastly cut back on energy use in response to its higher price (reflecting its increased scarcity), we have continued to use the water and air with abandon. We have not been induced to behave in ways that respect the increased scarcity of clean air and water.

The best-known proposal of an incentive approach to protecting air and water quality is that per-unit charges be set for the dumping of pollutants into the air or water. This would require both legislative action and regulatory implementation. Charges should approximately reflect the "opportunity cost" of those resources—that is, how valuable they are in other uses, such as commercial, recreational, and aesthetic uses. The charges should consequently be different for each major pollutant, depending on the regional conditions of air and water resources and the possible alternative uses to which they could be put.

Faced with the prospect of paying X dollars per unit for the disposal of a specific effluent into the water or emission into the air, a municipality or firm would have three choices: (1) paying that rate and maintaining the current level of discharge, (2) investing in equipment and processes to eliminate or clean up the discharge completely, (3) spending money to reduce or clean up most of the discharge while paying the set rate on any residual discharge. The decision would certainly vary among firms and industries, because the per-unit cost of reducing discharges of a pollutant varies greatly, depending on the type of product produced as well as the percentage of cleanup attempted.

In Chapter Three we described the decision-making process by which a firm seeking to maximize profits decides what and how to produce. We noted that as relative prices of inputs (resources) in production change, firms are induced to alter production in favor of the more abundant, less expensive resources and against those scarcer resources for which prices are rising. In fact, adequate competition among producers in the same product market forces individual firms to respond in this way. By paying attention to relative cost signals, the more adept managers are able to reduce costs and thus enjoy greater profits than the less adept decision makers. A system of effluent/emission charges would have a similar impact on decisions. Unless the charges were trivial, firms would have a strong cost/profit incentive to reduce their reliance on air and water disposal. Furthermore, the firms that could reduce discharges most inexpensively would have the strongest incentive to do so. (Whether asking polluters to pay for their discharges constitutes giving them a "license to pollute" will be dealt with shortly.)

A legitimate question arises about what should be done with revenues to be generated from effluent and emission charges.[1] Since the charge itself is set in part by placing a dollar value on the per-unit damages inflicted by the pollutant emitted, it seems most appropriate that revenues be used to further reduce pollution, to help people take protective measures against damage, or to indemnify them for the damages.[2] In some cases, especially when the source of the pollution is stationary, it may be possible to identify the particular individuals suffering damages and assess a dollar value for the damage. (In Japan, for instance, people living in high pollution areas who suffer from ailments aggravated by poor air or water quality can apply for compensation that is taken out of revenues from a tax on polluters.)[3] In other cases—for example, the damage done by motor vehicle emissions—identifying particular victims would be an impossible task.

Another possibility is that some portion of the revenues generated by charges could be returned to the firms paying the charges. Of course, in order for the charge to continue its effect of discouraging emissions, the return would have to be in the form of relief from some other business tax that is unrelated to specific firms' emissions levels.[4] Justification for an arrangement of tax relief in exchange for greater pollution control is

1. See Thomas C. Schelling, "Prices as Regulatory Instruments," in *Incentives for Environmental Protection,* ed. Thomas C. Schelling (Cambridge: MIT Press, 1983), pp. 22ff.

2. There would be one disadvantage of indemnifying people for damages suffered from pollution: it would eliminate an existing incentive for them to relocate where pollution damage is less severe. (Notice how people keep building on flood plains, knowing that guaranteed federal subsidies in the event of flood damage partially protect their investments.) It's not hard to see how social costs from pollution are reduced, for instance, if especially vulnerable members of the population choose to relocate in less polluted regions. By reducing their victims' incentive to move, indemnification would make the total damages from pollution greater than they otherwise would be. On the other hand, it's not clear why those already located in an area now being subjected to high pollution levels should have to bear the cost of their own relocation or of other measures they might take to reduce their vulnerability to damages. A workable solution to this dilemma might be awarding victims only partial indemnification unless they relocate to places with cleaner environments.

3. See Edwin S. Mills, *The Economics of Environmental Quality* (New York: W. W. Norton, 1978), pp. 263-64.

4. It's easy to see why rebates need not compromise the objective of reducing pollution levels. Suppose the Miller Company now pays effluent charges at the rate of twenty cents per pound of effluent, and runs up a total bill of $5,000 for the year. The government now offers to all medium-sized producers in the same industry a $2,000 rebate on their corporate profits tax. The effluent charge was intended to encourage firms to reduce their effluents. Will the prospect of a rebate weaken this incentive for the Miller Company? No, because the firm will get the $2,000 whether or not it reduces effluent levels; and its bill for effluent charges will be less—and profits, therefore, greater—if it can find a way to reduce the offending discharge at a cost of less than twenty cents per pound.

primarily political, the hope being that the prospect of some modest tax relief would reduce industry resistance to substituting an incentive system for the present approach of direct regulation.

There are a number of important arguments that favor replacing much of what is now attempted through law and regulation with this incentive approach to pollution control. By far the most weighty argument is that achieving any given environmental cleanup or protection goal will cost far less using the incentive approach. It is easy to see why. To date, the main approach of regulatory authorities has been to require that all firms be subject to the same effluent/emission standard. For example, all firms may be required to reduce by 80 percent the amount of BOD (biochemical oxygen demand) entering bodies of water they use. BOD measures organic wastes in terms of the demands that their breakdown puts on the oxygen levels in the water. (The more BOD released into water, the less oxygen remains for fish.) However, the same objective could be reached by inducing firms for whom BOD reduction is least costly to exceed the 80 percent reduction rate, while other firms for whom that degree of BOD reduction is very expensive achieve less than an 80 percent reduction. This is precisely what an effluent charge would do: encourage various degrees of BOD reduction among firms depending on the relative costs associated with their efforts. If charges are set at an appropriate level, the improvement in environmental quality would be identical to that achieved by current rules requiring uniform BOD reduction, but it would cost significantly less.

What is known about the cost advantages of using charges, one form of an incentive approach to pollution control? Data have been accumulating that demonstrate wide differences in the cost of pollution reduction across industries and for different levels of purity achieved. Figures 1 and 2 provide some striking examples of both. Although Figures 1 and 2 use data from 1973 and compare only two industries, the pollution abatement costs they show are very typical. Starting from a 70 percent reduction in BOD, pollution could be reduced by an additional pound for less than three cents in the beet-sugar refining industry compared with over fourteen cents in the petroleum refining industry (see dashed lines on the Figures). Other estimates comparing the financial burden of abatement across industries using the "best practicable technology standards" show that costs per kilogram of BOD removed may be *thirty times greater* in one industry than in another.[5]

5. See Winston Harrington and Alan J. Krupnick, "Stationary Source Pollution Policy and Choices for Reform," in *Environmental Regulation and the U.S. Economy*, ed. H. M. Peskin et al., *Resources for the Future* (Baltimore: The Johns Hopkins University Press, 1981), p. 109.

Figure 1.

Marginal Cost of BOD Discharge Reduction
by a Beet Sugar Refinery

Percentage reduction in discharge

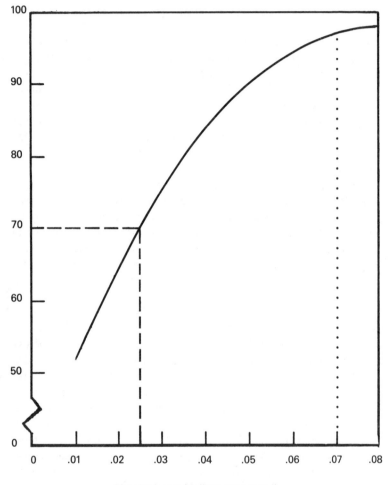

Marginal cost (dollars per pound)

Source: Clifford S. Russell, "Restraining Demand by Pricing Water Withdrawals and Wastewater Disposal" (prepared for presentation at a seminar on the Management of Water Supplies, University of East Anglia, Norwich, England, March 1973; processed).

Figure 2.

Marginal Cost of BOD Discharge Reduction in Petroleum Refining

Percentage reduction in discharge

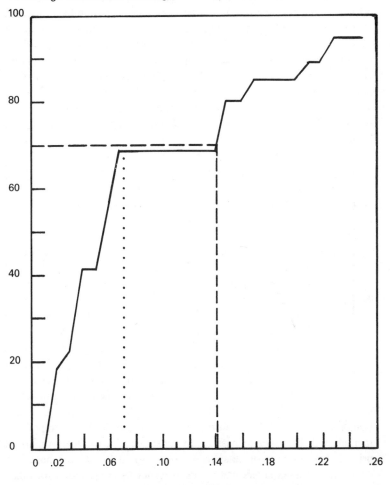

Marginal cost (dollars per pound)

Source: Clifford S. Russell, *Residuals Management in Industry: A Case Study of Petroleum Refining* (Johns Hopkins University Press for Resources for the Future, 1973).

The cost comparisons between beet-sugar refining and oil refining tell us that if reasonable water standards in a given locale require a reduction of one million pounds in BOD, then it would save nearly $108,000 in costs to encourage a beet-sugar refinery along the stream to do *all* the effluent reduction, rather than splitting the cleanup job between this refinery and a petroleum refinery. Effluent charges would have just this cost-saving effect by inducing the beet-sugar refinery to handle most of the BOD reduction. For example, an effluent charge of seven cents per pound of BOD would cause the beet-sugar refinery to reduce BOD discharge by about 97 percent, and the oil refinery by about 68 percent (see dotted lines on the Figures). Theoretically, a similar result could be achieved by setting stricter standards for beet-sugar refining than for oil refining. However, this would require that regulators setting standards be intimately acquainted with the comparative costs of pollution abatement for different industries and for many different firms within a particular industry. That information could only be gathered imperfectly and at very great cost. The beauty of charges is that decisions about how to reduce pollution are made at the level of each firm, according to their knowledge of the technologies, processes, and abatement costs peculiar to their method of production.

Let's consider a more comprehensive picture of the potential cost savings to be gained by substituting effluent/emission charges for uniform regulatory standards affecting air and water quality. A conservative estimate of the fifteen-year cost (beginning in 1975) of attaining already legislated environmental goals via mandated standards for air and water quality is $500 billion. Economists Allen Kneese and Charles Schultz suggest that the $500 billion expenditure could be cut by 40-50 percent if charges were used instead of uniform standards.[6] Such potential savings cannot be ignored, because they could be used to further improve environmental quality or to support other nonenvironmental programs that also have great private and social significance, such as health and education programs and services for the poor. Of course, firms in competitive markets will be eager to pass on to consumers (in the form of lower prices) their savings on abatement costs. So, it is into the hands of consumers and taxpayers that financial resources are released for other purposes when more cost-efficient pollution controls are employed.

6. See Allen V. Kneese and Charles L. Schultz, *Pollution, Prices and Public Policy* (Washington: The Brookings Institution, 1975), p. 81.

OTHER ADVANTAGES OF THE INCENTIVE
APPROACH USING CHARGES

In addition to direct cost savings, the incentive approach using charges has several other advantages over the direct regulatory approach. The first of these is often mistaken as a disadvantage—namely, that the charges paid by those firms continuing to use air and water for some waste disposal will be partially passed on to consumers in the form of higher prices. If we think of the discharge of pollutants as a "bad deed," then it seems unfair for the penalty (charges) to be borne by consumers rather than by the owners of the firm responsible for the deed. However, discharges of some kind must be recognized as an inevitable part of manufacturing processes. The choices firms make about this end of production are legitimately related to comparative costs, just as are the decisions they make about how to combine productive inputs like capital and labor, or steel and aluminum, or gas and electrical energy. When a firm finds that further reductions of its effluents or emissions are uneconomical, it will pay the charges for releasing a certain amount of waste into the air or water. These charges, like all production-related costs, *need* to be passed on in higher prices paid by consumers, so that consumers can respond in their purchases to the true scarcity of these products and services and of the resources used in their production.

Prior to the introduction of charges, a roll of white paper toweling, for instance, might cost the same as a roll of brown paper toweling. Given the apparent preference in this society for cleansing products that look "clean" because they are white, we can expect sales of white toweling to exceed sales of brown toweling. However, if charges are introduced, a price differential between the two will evolve, since the bleaching process involved in making the white toweling produces much more effluent.[7] The white toweling will become more expensive than the brown toweling, therefore inducing some consumers to switch. Society is better off when prices of white toweling go up, because this leads to fewer purchases and reduced output of a product whose excessive production fouls the water. And those who continue to buy white toweling will pay a price that reflects the increased burden its production puts on scarce water resources.

In earlier chapters we have shown how important it is that prices be allowed to convey to users the relative scarcity of a good or input. Thus, effluent charges function in the same way that oil prices do: they induce

7. See Kneese and Schultz, *Pollution, Prices and Public Policy*, p. 5.

us to behave in ways that are consistent with the degree of preciousness—that is, scarcity—of our environmental and other natural resources. The example just given clearly shows how charging producers for their use of air or water can generate some very useful information for consumers in the form of relative price changes. When producers do not pay for their use of communal resources, it takes very well-informed consumers to know how they might responsibly change their consumption patterns out of respect for environmental concerns. But when prices do reflect the total resource demands being made by the production and disposal of a good, then the consumer's desire to be "responsible" is made much easier. Shopping by comparing prices then turns out to be good for both the pocketbook and the environment.

In addition to reducing costs for environmental protection and improving the allocation of scarce environmental resources, charges offer a third important advantage over regulatory rules. This lies in the realm of technological advances in waste treatment and in production processes that minimize environmental damage. The existing regulatory process has focused primarily on the treatment of emissions or effluents to remove damaging substances. It has also involved the regulators in determining what is "the best adequately demonstrated control technology," in order to set technically achievable performance standards for new sources of pollutant discharges. However, those people in the best position to know the possible alternative strategies for meeting a performance standard and those motivated strongly to choose the most cost-efficient strategy are the producers themselves. When regulators prescribe a certain technology to meet a pollution-reduction performance standard, they remove the incentive that would otherwise be there to encourage producers to search out less expensive but equally successful solutions to meeting the same standard.

On the other hand, charges on pollutants would enable and encourage producers to look for the most cost-efficient ways to minimize pollutants discharged into the air or water. Their interest in effective, cost-saving methods would in turn stimulate technological advances and strong competition in industries supplying cleanup and pollution-control equipment. We can find a parallel in the rapid development of energy-saving technologies that high energy prices have elicited since the late 1970s. The astonishing success of market-driven energy conservation efforts is the reason the United States no longer finds itself "over the (OPEC) barrel." Furthermore, whereas companies that already meet current regulatory standards have no explicit incentives to further reduce discharges of pollutants, under a system of charges the financial incentive would continue to elicit technological advances capable of reducing effluents and emissions even below current standards.

There is a final argument in favor of using the incentive system—namely, the administrative simplicity of charges. A regulatory agency would be relieved of the need to know a great deal about production technologies in hundreds of different industries and thousands of different firms. The job of regulators would be twofold. First, they would have to estimate (or experiment to determine) the per-unit rates that would have to be charged for different types of pollutants, in order to induce a level of discharge that met desirable environmental standards. This is not a totally simple and inexpensive administrative task, but experts generally agree that it would be simpler, cheaper, and more effective than the present system. Second, regulators would have to devise methods for monitoring the compliance of firms and municipalities by requiring them to accurately meter (or otherwise assess) their discharge of effluents and emissions, on which they would pay the established rate per unit. (This is not unlike the IRS's task of monitoring the accuracy of self-reported income.) We can expect that a market would develop in devices that firms could use to measure discharges and that regulators could use to estimate degrees of compliance. (In some cases, the latter could conceivably be done with remote sensors rather than by on-site checks.)

Electric power plants provide an interesting example of the difficulties commonly associated with direct regulatory control.[8] By examining these problems, we can more fully appreciate some of the advantages just cited for using an incentive approach instead of direct controls. In 1973, the Environmental Protection Agency (EPA) had to set emission standards for power plants based on its determination of what was an "adequately demonstrated technology" for controlling the emission of sulfur dioxide. It argued for basing emissions standards on a technology that had been in use for three decades in some English and Japanese plants. Representatives of U.S. industry claimed that the control equipment used in these foreign firms was too expensive and unreliable. In reponse, the EPA eventually relaxed its standards, permitting power plants to substitute tall smokestacks (which dilute the pollutants into a greater volume of air) for the more expensive control equipment. EPA Administrator John R. Quarles, Jr., put his finger on the regulatory dilemma when he said that the choices were "this or nothing or a shutdown" of plants not able to meet EPA standards. The tall stack solution turned out to cause

8. See Kneese and Schultz, *Pollution, Prices and Public Policy*, p. 59.

other problems at greater distances from the source, the greatest of which was (and is) acid rain. This problem was complicated by the energy shortage. Consequently, a series of legislated steps was taken in the late 1970s requiring both new and existing electric utilities to switch from burning oil and gas to burning coal. Since burning coal releases more sulfur than does oil or gas, acid rain conditions have become further aggravated.

To review, the EPA had the task of determining feasible technologies. When its standards based on a particular technology met with industry resistance, it was forced to back down. Yet in this case as well as in most others, we could not expect the EPA to have the expertise needed to determine *the* environmentally desirable and financially feasible technology for all producers, especially since it is unlikely that this would be the same for each producer. If, instead, the EPA had set an emission charge that adequately reflected both nearby and distant damage (and if the EPA had likewise tackled the oil shortage problem with price or tax incentives to reduce oil use instead of mandates on types of fuels used), individual utilities would have had sufficient information about social and material costs to systematically tackle the multiple decisions they faced. Should they produce with oil, low-sulfur coal, or high-sulfur coal? Should they install equipment similar to that used by English and Japanese firms or instead build tall stacks? Should they make other production adjustments to reduce sulfur emissions, or should they simply pay the discharge fees, passing them on to electric consumers in higher prices? We would have expected their choices to vary according to the age of the facilities, geographic conditions, and other factors. We would also have expected cost and profit considerations to invigorate the search to develop alternative control technologies, ultimately achieving a still greater reduction in emissions at lower cost.

OTHER INCENTIVE-BASED APPROACHES

We have examined the case for using an incentive approach that relies on charges. There are two other types of incentive proposals: granting subsidies to those who install abatement equipment, and creating markets for discharge permits. We will see why only the latter enjoys widespread support among economists.

Since regulatory authorities already determine what amounts of discharges can safely be handled by regional air and water systems, they could sell rights to firms to discharge up to the maximum amount determined to be safe. Obviously, those firms for whom emission or effluent reduction is most costly would attempt to buy more permits than firms whose reduction costs are comparatively low. As circumstances changed—for instance, when a new firm wanted to locate in an area—it would buy permits from firms willing to give them up at the market-determined price. Industrial development would increase the demand for permits, thus driving up their price, while technical advances permitting lower pollution control costs would cause firms to sell off permits, thereby reducing the market price. The principal advantage of permits over administratively set charges is that regulatory authorities would not have to guess at the necessary charges to achieve targeted standards for effluence and emission. Instead, the cost of disposing pollutants into the water or air would simply take the form of a competitively determined market price paid for permits.

Charges set on emissions and effluents (or the prices paid for these in newly created permit markets) constitute disincentives to pollute, thereby stimulating efforts to abate or clean up the offending flows of waste. Why not use positive incentives instead, granting subsidies to those who abate? Because this approach is not as attractive as it might first appear. For one thing, offering subsidies means having to finance them with higher taxes elsewhere. In addition, there are other problems—major ones—with the subsidy approach.

First, some sort of emission/effluent benchmark must be arrived at, with subsidies granted to those reducing emissions below this level. Of course, the largest subsidies would then go to the worst offenders, some of whom had dragged their feet for years rather than reduce their discharges at a comparatively modest cost. Furthermore, a period of discussion and public hearings on the matter of the benchmark could itself produce an incentive for firms to temporarily increase discharges so that they could subsequently be paid for reducing waste disposal below the established benchmark.

Second, unlike emissions charges, subsidies do not produce correct price signals to consumers. When subsidies are granted to producers, the consumers of bleached paper towels, coal-generated electricity, and food produced through heavy use of chemical fertilizers and herbicides (on land with heavy soil runoffs into streams) will not directly pay for the burden their consumption puts on water and air resources, nor will they be induced by relative price changes to search for products whose production causes less pollution.

Third, subsidies have a long history of inefficient administration. The best example in this country comes from the subsidies that have been granted to municipalities for construction of waste treatment plants. For the most part these subsidies were granted on a "first come, first served" basis, with no special consideration given to where the investment would do the most to reduce environmental damage from inadequately treated sewage. Consequently, about 60 percent of the grants went to towns with 25,000 or fewer inhabitants, who together accounted for only about 30 percent of the U.S. urban population.[9] Furthermore, while much attention was given to building facilities, no attention was paid to ensuring that the facilities were used efficiently for maximum cleanup. (This is a reminder that less developed countries are not the only ones to overindulge in building physically impressive projects while underinvesting in the delivery of the services and the upkeep of facilities.) The cost of this massive subsidy program proved to be very high relative to the modest results achieved.

Taken together, these three arguments explain why subsidies are such an unattractive alternative to an incentive-based scheme that relies on either emission/effluent charges or marketed permits.

DISCHARGE PERMITS COMPARED WITH MORE FAMILIAR LICENSES

The incentive approach to environmental protection—whether via charges or permits—often strikes ordinary citizens as quite bizarre, if not immoral. Our current regulatory approach says, "You may not put more than X amount of a pollutant into the air or water." And if you are caught in violation, the law prescribes penalties. This prohibition of certain activities puts the weight of law behind the stigma that society apparently wishes to attach to polluting. The substitution of charges or permits for legal sanctions would *appear* to remove much of the stigma attached to dumping discharges into the air and water. Perhaps this is why many people, upon first hearing about the proposal of charges, react by exclaiming, "It's a license to pollute!"

Just how strange is the idea of selling permits to reduce pollution? We can learn a great deal about this approach by comparing and contrasting it with the familiar hunting or fishing license. The purpose of these sports licenses is to keep the kill or catch within sustainable limits. The act of hunting or fishing itself is most often thought of as morally neutral unless it involves cruelty or endangers species. Similarly, the purpose of discharge permits is to control morally neutral activities which if done in excess would jeopardize human and animal life or diminish enjoyment and other human uses of the same body of water or air. What dis-

9. See Kneese and Schultz, *Pollution, Prices and Public Policy*, p. 36.

tinguishes a discharge permit from a fishing license is that the purpose of the actual fee set for the discharge permit is to induce restricted use of the water or air for dumping purposes, whereas the fee for a fishing license is primarily a tax designed to raise revenue. Thus price would serve this limiting function in the case of discharge permits, whereas direct limits on the catch rather than the fees for the fishing licenses themselves usually serve to restrict the number of fish caught for food and sport.

Another difference between discharge permits and fishing and hunting licenses is a consequence of the difference just mentioned. While fishing and hunting licenses are priced low enough for most people who want them to afford them, discharge permits would be quite expensive, and the costs of alternative measures for reducing discharges would also be quite high. In this way, the cost of using environmental resources becomes as explicit as other costs of doing business, and the strength of consumer demand for a service or product will determine a firm's ability to pay the discharge fees and abatement costs.

Despite these differences, the parallels between common sports licenses and discharge permits should help us realize that permits are not such a strange idea. Consequently, we may be less inclined to decry the suggestion that some sort of quasi-market incentives be used to protect air and water quality. But are discharge permits licenses to commit the immoral act of polluting? As we have seen earlier, pollution—like the overfishing that endangers certain species and depletes total numbers—results from the *excessive* use of air or water resources. (Of course, some wastes are extremely toxic even at low levels of concentration. In such cases, an outright ban rather than a permit system is obviously necessary.) Damages usually result when waste disposal in the aggregate exceeds a particular level. If this is the case, then disposal by one person or firm cannot by itself be called moral or immoral. Consequently, setting a fee for permission to discharge into the air or water is not "a license to pollute." Discharge permits are not official sanctions of immoral behavior but rather cost-effective devices to keep the use of precious common resources down to levels that will enable these resources to serve multiple purposes into the distant future.

CONCERNS ABOUT THE EFFECT OF THE INCENTIVE APPROACH ON THE ECONOMY AT LARGE

A whole host of questions may be raised about the larger consequences of an incentive approach to pollution control: what will be the impact on inflation, unemployment, investment, the GNP, and the foreign trade balance? We do know that pollution control, by whatever approach, can be expected in the short run to raise domestic price levels, thereby discouraging exports and stimulating imports (i.e., hurting the balance of trade). However, since an incentive approach offers great cost savings for any given amount of pollution control, inflation and adverse effects on foreign trade should be less than with a regulatory approach.

Whatever the approach taken to environmental protection, if foreign firms are not required to pay permit fees for their own waste disposal into the air and water, their products—sold at lower prices—can threaten domestic employment. Nations concerned about pollution at home may, therefore, find it in their own interest to cooperate in establishing international standards and approaches to environmental protection. (They will also want to consider applying an incentive approach to dealing with pollution—like acid rain—that crosses international borders.) Concern for protecting local employment, as well as for preventing local damage done by pollution coming from sources outside a region, have likewise been important reasons why state and regional actions to protect air and water have been coordinated at the federal level.

The net effects of pollution control on investment, the GNP, and unemployment are less certain than their impact on prices and trade. Investment in pollution control equipment itself will, of course, increase, but overall investment may decrease. However, overall investment levels are adversely affected by the current regulatory approach, which requires firms contemplating expansion to produce all sorts of environmental documentation before construction is approved. This can result in delays of several years and sometimes cancellation of investment plans. The incentive approach to pollution control would require very little direct intervention and authorization of investment projects—hence the adverse effect on timing and volume of investment should be less marked than under current policy.

It is also probable that an incentive approach would reduce the regulatory risks that producers face under the existing regime. Currently, a particular type of pollution control device suddenly becomes outdated when the EPA determines a better technology to be "adequately demonstrated," or when new rules are declared for the granting of construction permits. Consequently, firms may delay or cancel investment plans for fear of the financial risks associated with such an unpredictable regulatory climate. Again, the incentive approach will do less harm to investment plans because the choice of technology (and the balance between abatement and cleanup or payment of the emission/effluent charge) is left up to individual firms. With the incentive approach businesses have greater control of production processes and hence can better predict financial outcomes, which together favor higher investment levels.

Whether we should worry much about lowered rates of investment under the direct regulatory approach compared with potentially higher levels via the incentive approach depends in part on our assessment of how important long-run economic growth is (a subject to be taken up in Chapter Nine). However, in the short run it is clear that maintaining high investment levels is important, because the economic expansion thus supported and stimulated can get unemployment levels down and keep them down. Investment that raises productivity can also act as a damper on inflation.

So, while significant pollution control cannot be undertaken without some adverse consequences for price levels, foreign trade, and the GNP, a changeover to the incentive approach to regulation can be expected to mitigate the damage. This is extremely important, because high unemployment and high inflation have bred increasing popular opposition to environmental regulation. If it can be shown that an approach exists which would produce the same or even better environmental quality at great cost savings—with fewer adverse effects on prices and jobs—then the political feasibility of maintaining adequate environmental protection will improve. This is why the incentive approach is gaining favor with environmentalists.

HARD EVIDENCE ON POLLUTION CONTROL RESULTS USING THE INCENTIVE APPROACH, AND SOME TENTATIVE STEPS IN THAT DIRECTION

Having examined some of the worries frequently expressed about an incentive-based approach to pollution control, a final pair of questions deserves attention. First, is there any hard evidence that the incentive approach has been successfully used? Second, what steps, if any, have been taken toward applying the incentive approach in U.S. environmental regulation? Happily, we do have evidence from a number of countries—including France, Great Britain, Holland, and Czechoslovakia—that by the early 1970s were developing or using effluent charges.[10] During the 1960s, the French were notably unsuccessful in their use of direct regulatory controls to reduce pollution, but this situation was turned around dramatically in the early 1970s, when French river-basin agencies began to collect charges on polluters.

10. See William Q. Baumol and Wallace E. Oates, *Economics, Environmental Policy, and the Quality of Life* (Englewood Cliffs, N.J.: Prentice-Hall, 1979), pp. 256ff.

The most famous example of successful application of the charges approach comes from the Ruhr Basin of Germany. A system of water control management using charges was introduced prior to World War II. One of the world's largest concentrations of industry is located in the Ruhr Basin, accounting for 40 percent of all Germany's industrial capacity. In fact, the volume of effluents there *exceeds* the average flow of river water in the basin during the low-flow period. Nevertheless, with the help of effluent charges, the quality of water in this district has been high enough to support fishing and other recreational uses of the waters.

The United States has only recently taken tentative steps in the direction of using an incentive approach (other than subsidies) in environmental regulation. In 1979, the EPA introduced two new regulatory policies: the "bubble" and offsets. Under the "bubble," a factory that has more than one source of a particular emission may meet environmental standards if all the sources taken together do not exceed regulatory limits. Previously, each individual source was required to meet the standards. Thus, this policy—which figuratively draws a bubble around the entire factory and counts total emissions from that bubble—enables a firm to cut back on emissions in that part of the production process where it is least costly to do so, while continuing to emit waste at relatively higher levels where the alternatives are very expensive. Because the "bubble" policy is specific to a firm, it does not eliminate excessive control costs associated with requiring both a petroleum refinery and a beet-sugar processing plant to meet the same percentage reduction in effluents.

The offsets policy applies to firms that would like to build new factories or expand existing ones, enabling these firms to do so if they are able to correspondingly offset new emissions by reduction from existing sources. This usually takes place within a single firm. Occasionally, however, a firm has negotiated with municipalities and other polluters, paying them to reduce their pollution emissions sufficiently to offset the firm's new emissions.

It is apparent that neither of these policies constitutes a full-blown adoption of the incentive approach. Nonetheless, they both move in that direction and afford some opportunity to achieve existing environmental goals at lower costs. Unfortunately, little use has been made of "bubble" and offsets plans because of the need for expensive negotiations and the delays involved in meeting many regulatory requirements. Consequently, the savings on pollution control have been far less than those that would be generated by a more thoroughgoing conversion to charges or sale of permits.

THE ECONOMIC SOLUTION AND MORAL CONCERNS

If, by our discussion of incentive-based pollution controls, we seem to have stripped environmental concerns of moral content, this is not the case. Instead, we have shown why economic analysis of environmental issues may move moral decisions to a different point—away from individual choices about discharge and toward collective decisions about resource use. After all, pollution is primarily a problem of aggregates, requiring solutions at that level. So, rather than condemning all discharge as the product of immoral, self-interested behavior, we can see it as one of the multiple uses to which our environment may presently be put, but which must be limited.

The moral issue then becomes one of assessing the proper balance to be achieved among the various uses for air and water (as well as other natural resources such as wilderness, prairie lands, etc.). For instance, do we treat a stream just like an efficiently run sewer, with no attempt to protect its use for recreation and for wildlife (whether or not each of the species now supported by it has known importance to human life or aesthetic value)? Christians who take seriously their responsibility as stewards of the earth they've inherited will answer, "No, certainly not!" They may well disagree, however, on the inventory of essential material and symbolic purposes that ought to be served by environmental resources. For instance, to what extent should preservation of nature prevail over creative human utilization of natural resources?

As a control technique, the incentive approach to environmental protection is largely morally neutral. It does not involve sanctioning a social crime, but rather limiting behavior that in large amounts causes damage. (Although some authors have supported the incentive approach over direct regulatory controls on the grounds of greater freedom of choice, this distinction seems to lack a strong defense.) What the incentive approach does offer is the prospect of great cost savings in the achievement and protection of any desired level of environmental quality. As we've noted earlier in this chapter, this is no small monetary sum. Furthermore, the savings could be used to pursue a number of high moral purposes, one of which is certainly environmental protection at even higher levels than we now achieve using the regulatory approach.

Of course, cost saving in environmental control will not automatically be converted to use for high moral purposes—such as programs to reduce poverty, to expand access to education and the arts, and to further protect environmental resources for future generations. So, even if a system of disposal charges is widely adopted, Christians who want to see certain social values supported will have to apply their gifts of moral persuasion to the continual debates about the best allocation of these savings.

As we have seen, putting a price on air and water use is not the moral issue; deciding *what* price to charge is, however, heavily laden with values. A system of charges would vastly reduce the complexity of environmentally responsible shopping and producing, and would thereby enable us to give more thoughtful consideration to the issues surrounding aggregate uses of our environmental resources.

Questions for Further Consideration

1. The viewpoint expressed in this chapter is much less alarmist than that of some prominent secular and Christian writers. Read, for example, the quotation from Wes Granberg-Michaelson at the opening of the chapter. Is the cure for pollution less industrialization (or less "civilization"), stricter legal controls on profit-seeking behavior, greater encouragement of selflessness and conservation ethics, a new incentive-based approach to pollution control, or something else?

2. What does it mean to be an "environmentally responsible" consumer? How can this goal be balanced against necessary and stewardly concerns for nutrition, budgetary limits, and preparation and disposal time? How is the task sometimes made easier or more difficult?

3. Has economists' predilection for market solutions removed crucial moral implications from their analysis of the environment?

4. If a system of charges were instituted for most effluents and emissions, what would be the best use of the revenues generated?

CHAPTER SEVEN

Land Use: One Issue in Natural Resource Policy

What's wrong, according to critics, with our present use of land and natural resources? . . . It is alleged that we are cutting down forests, pumping oil, mining groundwater, overfishing the oceans, paving over farmland, and destroying the natural fertility of the soil.

Gordon C. Bjork, *Life, Liberty, and Property*

With frequently local land use policies and no clearly defined sets of national or state policies for shaping land use patterns, the nation aimlessly consumes its scarce land resources and ignores the important long-run implications of crisis-oriented, case-by-case land use decision making.

D. E. Dowall, in *Land Use Policy Debate in the U.S.*

From the standpoint of present sufficiency, little evidence suggests that a true resource problem (of food producing land) exists and government intervention is warranted.

Owen Furuseth and John T. Pierce,
Agricultural Land in an Urban Society

In the late twentieth century more than in any previous time, concerns are being raised about the rate at which humans are consuming the earth's resources—nonrenewable ones like mineral deposits, agricultural land, and areas of great natural beauty, as well as renewable resources like forests, fisheries, air, and water. Of course, increasing scarcities of some important resources have occurred before, such as that of whale oil, the major source of lighting fuel in the mid-nineteenth century. But historically only one or two such resources have been scarce at any given time. Furthermore, concerns over remaining supplies of these scarce resources have faded as improved transportation channels have brought in more remotely located resources to alleviate local and regional scarcities, and as rising resource prices have prompted the development of new technology that has brought substitutes within economic reach. (Such was the case when whale oil was replaced by the kerosene refined from newly discovered petroleum deposits.) What is new in the late twentieth century is a widespread pessimism about the capacity of the earth and its finite resources to meet increasing human needs and wants. World population growth, while it appears to be slowing, still promises to increase demands on resources. Rising personal incomes also add to the demands made on basic resources.

Assessments about the seriousness of the dangers posed by higher demands on limited resources vary greatly, depending on the assessor's degree of optimism or pessimism about the rate of future technical progress. Is it a near certainty or only a false hope that technology will continue to introduce substitutes, based on renewable resources, for products and services now produced with rapidly diminishing nonrenewable resources? While the popular media often bring "doom and gloom" projections to their audience's attention, professional economists as a group tend to be optimistic about continued technical progress and the substitution of more abundant resources for increasingly scarce ones.

The pessimists point out that technical "alternatives" to scarce resources have often put additional stress on the natural environment. For example, the scarcity of fertile soil has made pesticides and herbicides attractive as ways to increase crop yields per acre, and energy from nuclear plants relieves some of the burden on dwindling coal and oil reserves. Yet large pesticide and herbicide residues can contaminate water systems and build up to dangerous levels in the food chains of humans and animals, and the improper disposal of nuclear waste poses other dangers. In response to this criticism of their "naive" trust in technical progress, economists point out that every technical change has some adverse side effects. The best remedy for these effects, they say, is not to cap technology and restrain economic growth, but rather to introduce control mechanisms that minimize the social costs of growth, especially controls that rely on self-enforcing economic incentives.

Theologically minded critics of technical progress most often point to the danger of what amounts to a faith in human remedies that replaces repentance and trust in divine remedies. These critics sometimes interpret the natural and social costs of technical change as evidence of the inherent folly of an approach that they believe is based on incomplete human knowledge and the inordinate desire to exercise "control." And yet a balance sheet should not be judged by the negative side of the ledger alone, without thought to whether benefits may outweigh costs. Nor is it fair to assume that the drive toward technical progress is inspired more by hubris and greed than by a deeply imbedded human desire—modeled after the example of the Creator—to know, create, and share the fruits of these efforts with others.

Given the technical complexity of this debate about limited resources, and the difficulty of discerning the boundary between facts and the basic predispositions of futurists toward optimism or pessimism, what we attempt in this chapter is a more limited examination of one key scarce resource—namely, land. Land-use policy is a heated subtopic of the larger question of good social management of finite resources. Land is a multifaceted resource: its beauty inspires poetry, its allocation was a key element of Mosaic law, and its ownership and use have triggered many personal, political, and international disputes throughout the ages. It is the key resource for food production, and it is also important as housing sites for the world's peoples. An examination of land-use issues will equip readers to understand the problems with—and solutions to—the scarcity of other basic resources.

HISTORIC REFLECTIONS ON THE FAIRNESS OF LAND ALLOCATION AND PRIVATE OWNERSHIP

Land and other resources imbedded in the earth constitute endowments received by each generation. Because they do not create these resources, humans have long reflected more about fairness in land ownership than they have about fairness in the ownership of goods produced with a person's own skill and capital resources.[1] In the Judeo-Christian tradition, a distinction was made between individuals' outright ownership of personal property and their stewardship of land resources for a limited period. However, the distinction between stewards and owners was not a perfect one in terms of the degree of control they were permitted to exercise over the use of their properties. Mosaic law and the teaching of the prophets demanded that the government, priests, and the poor be supported out of incomes generated by *all* resources—whether they were leased, as in the case of all agricultural land, or owned outright, as in the case of a shop.

Post-biblical Western thought about private ownership of land ranges from the highly individualistic view espoused by John Locke to the social contract view advanced by utilitarians and others. Locke appreciated the fact that private ownership can benefit society as a whole because of the incentive owners have to make their assets productive. Locke also thought that private property was directly related to maintaining liberty. He believed that liberty could be preserved only where people had the right to apply their energies and creativity to work (or consumption) and to keep any assets thereby generated. Land, of course, is an asset whose

---

1. For a more extensive historical treatment of property rights, see chap. 4 of Gordon C. Bjork's *Life, Liberty, and Property: The Economics and Politics of Land-Use Planning and Environmental Controls* (Lexington, Mass.: D. C. Heath, 1980).

value is "created" by its owner only to the extent that he or she clears it, drains it, or otherwise makes it economically useful.

Locke's view was vulnerable to criticism principally because his defense of private land ownership takes little account of the plight of generations who may have no access to land even though it might have been distributed fairly among members of an earlier generation (which Locke assumed as a starting point). He also ignored the ways in which one person's use of his or her own land might interfere with the neighbor's use of adjoining property (e.g., problems with noise, unsightliness, etc.).

Utilitarians defended the importance of private property on the basis of a hypothetical social contract to which people implicitly subscribe. Citizens are permitted by their society to retain ownership over property only because it (1) enhances total social well-being by maintaining incentives for people to put the land to productive use, and (2) reduces friction that would otherwise arise over the best use of something collectively owned.

Both these views of property—the Lockean emphasis on the preservation of individual liberty through private property ownership, and the utilitarian emphasis on the social benefits of private property—have helped form American attitudes toward land ownership and the legal framework for it. The utilitarian influence is evident in the Homestead Act of 1862, which granted possession rights only after a homesteader had lived on a tract of land and made it productive for at least five years. Thus homesteaders' rights to the land were based on their having invested themselves in the land's development, which simultaneously made a social contribution in the form of additional products from the land. Other examples of the conditional character of property rights in the United States include "adverse possession," by which a seven-year occupancy of land gives the occupant the right to file for title to that land, even if it is actually owned by someone else; and the public use of eminent domain, by which rights-of-way have been given to railroad and canal companies with only nominal compensation made to the property owners.

It is clear that American legal tradition has implicitly accepted the notion that private property ownership is an embodiment of personal liberty, but with the expectation and limitation that private property arrangements must continue to benefit the general public more than some alternative would (such as public ownership of certain sites necessary for the provision of public services like education, roads, sewage disposal, etc.).

Despite its evident commitment to market systems for handling most production and resource allocation, the United States has maintained two types of land ownership for many years. One third of U.S. land is owned and managed by governments for use as pasture, forest, and recreation sites, while the remaining two-thirds is owned by private individuals or corporations. Does this system of private ownership continue to produce the social benefits claimed for it by Aristotle, Locke, Hume, and others? Or should private owners' rights be further circumscribed by land use regulations (such as zoning), taxation, or public condemnation of certain rights and appropriation of certain lands?

Many would answer "yes" to the question about land-use regulation, because they believe that unencumbered private ownership too often violates the ethics of conservation and of equity. After all, they worry, isn't there a danger that profit-seeking developers will aggravate existing world hunger problems by too rapidly converting rich, food-producing lands into housing tracts? Wouldn't such development leave us in a terrible bind when the world's food supplies later proved more inadequate than ever to meet food needs at prices affordable by the poor? Won't struggling farmers be forced to choose between continued depletion of fertile soil, with attendant decreases in crop yields, or selling their land at a profit for urban development? In order to address these questions, we need to examine how markets allocate land among various uses, what unacceptable side-effects may result from unencumbered land markets, and what public policies have been adopted to dictate, guide, or induce land uses more consistent with social well-being.

MARKETS IN LAND—HOW THEY WORK

Privately owned land, like anything else bought and sold on the market, is subject to the dictates of changing supply and demand conditions. The total stock of land is, of course, fixed, but its availability to various markets depends on existing technologies and the costs of inputs needed to convert the land to economic uses. Those costs may include draining or terracing land for agricultural use, or building transportation and utility infrastructures for industrial, commercial, and residential use.

Demand for land is influenced by population, income levels, tastes, and the availability of substitutes. These factors affect the relative demands for different uses of land, such as for industrial sites, housing, food production, or recreation. So, for instance, the vast increases in North American agricultural yields per acre achieved in the 1950s, 1960s, and early 1970s had the effect of decreasing demand for agricultural land. This was partially offset by two factors raising world demand for food and hence for food-producing land: population increases and income growth. But income and population growth in the United States also contributed to increased demand both for goods requiring production sites and for housing. In fact, since the 1930s this demand has caused land to be put to urban uses much faster than to agricultural uses.[2] Furthermore, the most dramatic change to have affected demand for land put to urban use in North America is the automobile. Cars have made it possible for people to live much farther away from their work than was possible when they depended primarily on walking or using horses or urban public transport.

These changing factors of demand have been the principal influences on the price of land and its shifting use. As we've noted in earlier chapters, the price that people are willing and able to pay for a certain good or service indicates the relative value they attach to it. Thus, when people are willing to spend more on land for housing than on land for agriculture, and are able to pay prices sufficient to cover the cost of the land's conversion to urban use (including streets and sewers), land is converted from agricultural to residential use. The same applies to conversion of land from residential to industrial use. When demands for industrial output warrant prices for production sites greater than the prices that householders are willing to pay to keep land in residential use, land is put to that more intensive use.

The price of land, as determined by supply and demand conditions, reflects what the highest bidder expects to earn in the form of economic returns on that piece of land. The highest bid may also reflect the psychological value of land ownership per se and its noneconomic use value. So, for instance, a farmer who derives no special psychological benefits from land ownership and use but who expects to be able to earn one hundred dollars per acre in net revenues (what remains after paying all production costs including the farmer's own labor) would be willing to pay a maximum rent of one hundred dollars for an acre of land. On the other hand, a commercial enterprise might be able to offer one thousand dollars annual rent for a one-acre site based on the greater economic productivity of the land in commercial use.

Both of these rental rates based on net revenues can be converted to the maximum prices that the farmer and the commercial entrepreneur would be willing to pay for this acre of land. For instance, assuming that both the farmer and the prospective commercial buyer have alternative investments open to them for an annual return of ten percent, the farmer would be willing to pay a maximum approaching one thousand dollars as the

---

2. See Raleigh Barlowe, *Land Resource Economics: The Economics of Real Estate,* 3d ed. (Englewood Cliffs, N.J.: Prentice-Hall, 1978), pp. 49-50.

projected number of years he/she expected to farm the land rose toward some large number. The commercial entrepreneur would be willing to pay a figure approaching ten thousand dollars for the same property. These prices are arrived at by "capitalizing" the expected net returns from the land. In this case, the farmer would be outbid, and the market would therefore allocate this parcel of land to commercial use. Notice that society gains an advantage of nine thousand dollars when the land is allocated to commercial use, since the net value of its commercial output exceeds the net value of its potential agricultural output.

The same sort of allocation toward higher valued use occurs if a bid for residential use of a tract of land exceeds the bid for agricultural use. Here a householder (or a developer) offers a price for the land equal to the capitalized value of the net return that property would earn for its owner in rents upon conversion to residential use. Its capitalized rental price is one measure of the land's value (an opportunity cost) to the owner if he or she occupies the land after building on it. Again, when that offer price exceeds what the farmer is able to offer for the land, the parcel goes to the more intensive residential use and thereby increases the total social value of output produced on that land.

THE POTENTIAL VIRTUES OF MARKET ALLOCATION OF LAND AMONG COMPETING USES

What makes such a system of market allocation of the private property rights to land so attractive? First, as we've just seen, the market allocates land among alternate uses—recreational, agricultural, residential, and commercial—in such a way that the total value of output on the land is maximized. In addition to allocating land among a variety of current uses, such a system also allocates land between present and future use. How does this happen? A farm acreage may presently be worth more in residential use than in agricultural use, but promise large returns in farming if future food demand per acre rises relative to housing demand per acre. If those returns are projected to rise dramatically, if they are expected in the not-too-distant future, and if they can reasonably be capitalized at low rates of interest, then it will pay the farm owner, or a prospective buyer, to keep the land in agricultural use rather than converting it to urban uses.

Beyond this, markets in private property rights to land also produce incentives, rewarding owners who either develop lands for their most socially valued use (as measured by financial returns) or sell them to someone who will. Suppose Carol and Al buy a farm which is well beyond the fringes of an urban area. The price paid at the time of purchase is based on the maximum income it can provide its owners in agricultural use. Later, as the city expands nearer their farm, the offer price for it goes up, reflecting its increased value in urban uses. Carol and Al will then have every financial incentive to sell the land at a value usually far in excess of the net returns it promises in farming. Alternatively, consider the case of Jim, a householder with an empty lot conveniently located in a densely populated residential district. A price bid for his lot by a commercial buyer who wants to build a convenience store on it may now exceed any price a residential buyer would willingly offer him. If so, Jim has an incentive either to go into the convenience store business or to sell the lot to someone who can extract greater value by servicing harried last-minute shoppers than by living on the land.

It is this prodding of owners to put their land to the most productive, socially valued uses that really justifies society's granting exclusive property rights to individuals. If such rights instead made the individual better off at the expense of society, private property rights would not be sustained. But if by granting private property rights to individuals society is made better off because of the incentive owners face to increase output from the land, then society can willingly provide for and protect private rights to the land.

Another virtue of private rights to land is that once they are established, conflicts over how the land will be used are likely to be less frequent than they would be under a system of communal ownership and management. When collectivities are faced with diverse ideas about whether land should be allocated for windbreaks or crops or housing, they must resolve these differences by fiat or vote. But in a free land market, individual landowners are not forced to haggle with others over how best to use the land or to follow the dictates of political leaders or popular majorities. Instead, they enjoy the right to do with their land what they please, which vastly simplifies the decision-making process. Societies accept this when they believe that market forces are strong enough to guarantee that landowners will pay sufficient attention to the wants and needs expressed by people who do not own land but who are willing and able to pay for goods and services produced with the assistance of land. However, in societies where land is the principal asset, this tolerance for private landholding (and the attendant reduction in conflicts over its use) can be maintained only if land and incomes are reasonably well distributed. Historically, where there has been great inequality of land ownership and incomes, social conflict has been rampant. Central America is a dramatic current example of conflict born of extreme inequality in landholdings.

One final virtue of private property rights to land is that they minimize the need for social (traditional or criminal) incentives or sanctions as devices to get people to use their land to produce socially desired types and amounts of goods and services. When land is collectively owned, public ridicule may be the chief means of dealing with laggards, and criminal fines may apply to those who improperly use land for personal advantage rather than for prescribed types of communal output. But when markets exist, getting land to be put to its best use is a self-enforcing process. Changes in market production are the result of evaluations of supply-and-demand conditions made by those close to available cost and output data, whose livelihoods depend on their ability to accurately interpret and efficiently respond to that data. Landowners will usually do what buyers want without coercion.

FAILURES AND DISTORTIONS IN LAND MARKETS

Having described the benefits expected from private property rights to land and from the allocation of these rights through markets, we need to examine the ways in which land markets can "fail"—either in terms of their efficiency or equity. These turn out to be the very same ways that markets in any good or service can fail, but here we are interested in the implications for land-use policy, which is comprised of various interventions meant to prevent and correct market failure. First, there may be "spillover effects"—either positive or negative—when owners' choices about land use create side effects that either encroach upon or enhance neighbors' use of their land. Negative spillover effects of agricultural land use may include poor clearing and cropping practices, which increase the incidence of flooding and so reduce the productivity of nearby farms. A negative spillover effect is also involved when an urban developer does not include among the costs of land development the impact that high density housing can have on neighbors' peace and quiet, safety, and aesthetic environment.

Whenever negative spillover effects are significant, a certain type of production will exceed its social optimum (the amount determined when both private and social costs are compared with benefits). For instance, when too much land susceptible to large-scale erosion is used for food production, or when too many high-rise apartments are built in areas where the social costs of such high-density living are great, land is not being used in socially optimal ways. Various government regulations of land use have been prompted by the public's desire to reduce negative spillover effects. These efforts range from the establishment of rural soil banks to urban zoning. (We take a look at zoning in the next section.)

Positive spillover effects (sometimes called "external benefits") also affect the workings of land markets. For example, forested land may be owned and exploited for the value of its timber. That same forest may also provide important ecological benefits to the surrounding area, such as flood control and animal habitat. However, unless special steps are taken to provide forest owners with an economic return in exchange for their maintenance of these ecological services, it is likely that decisions the owners make about forest and land management will be based primarily on timber profits.

External benefits also exist when city residents enjoy the beauty of an agricultural greenbelt surrounding their city. In this case, too, an unencumbered land market would ignore these benefits, since they do not generate additional income for the farmers above the net value of their crops. We could expect many farmers in this situation to sell their land for urban development at a price that simply exceeds its value in crops, without requiring payment for the inevitable destruction of environmental (greenbelt) amenities. Thus external benefits that go financially unrewarded will almost certainly dwindle.

Negative and positive spillover effects from certain land uses create situations in which land markets can fail naturally to give us the most socially efficient allocation of resources. Public tax and pricing policies can also unintentionally distort land markets in such a way that land is allocated to less valued uses.[3] Favorable tax treatment of house ownership is an important example of this (and may reflect a peculiarly American belief in the economic, political, and even moral superiority of home ownership over renting). For instance, interest payments on home mortgages may be deducted from income that is to be federally taxed. The size of the tax advantage of home purchase increases with the person's income tax bracket. This tax treatment strongly favors landed home ownership over rental of housing units.

There are other tax benefits of home ownership. If Sally, a single professional woman, decides to rent an apartment and use her savings to make financial investments, she will have to pay income taxes on the interest earnings from those investments. On the other hand, Mary and her family will not have to pay any income taxes on the equivalent of interest income they "earn" on the investment they make in their own house, since they are not taxed for the consumption benefits they enjoy from occupying their own house and the land on which it sits. In addition, Sally will have to pay capital gains taxes on the sale of any appreciated financial assets, whereas Mary and her family will pay no taxes on capital

3. For a good summary, see chaps. 6 and 7 of Bjork's *Life, Liberty, and Property.*

gains from the sale of their home as long as they reinvest those gains quickly in another house of equal or greater value.

These various tax advantages of home ownership constitute an important factor contributing to urban sprawl. Without such indirect subsidies, people in need of housing would be more likely to rent, and those buying houses would be more inclined to buy small houses on small tracts of land. Cities would be more compact, because less land would be required both for housing itself and for roads, parking spaces, and so forth; and consequently, the pressure to convert agricultural land to urban uses would be less.

While special tax treatment favors rapid urban expansion, it is also true that the ways in which public utility prices are set further aggravate urban sprawl. Frequently, newly constructed schools, streets, and public utility systems serving new residents on the urban periphery are financed partially by taxes paid by those already living in the urban area. Furthermore, user charges sometimes also fail to reflect the extra costs associated with serving the newest residents. Taken together, the tax structure and utility prices have the effect of increasing the net attractiveness of owning property in new residential areas at the expense of the older areas. Of course, such an economic tilt in favor of residential expansion adds to the rates at which farms are converted to urban uses, since favorable taxes and utility prices for urban land far outweigh the positive impact of agricultural price supports on farm retention.

ZONING—A REMEDY FOR LAND MARKET IMPERFECTIONS?

These natural and administratively induced imperfections in land markets have been the basis for regulatory interventions in land use. Zoning is one such regulatory device that has been widely used by U.S. counties and municipalities.[4] Its historic purpose has been primarily to insure compatible uses of neighboring properties, thereby vastly reducing negative spillover effects. More recently, proposals have arisen to employ zoning of agricultural land as a device to protect croplands from encroaching urban sprawl. Zoning deserves more critical examination than the general public has given it. What attention it usually receives often comes only from those who expect to benefit from or be hurt by proposed rezonings or variances.

Although zoning is commonly employed to regulate land use, it is

4. For a critical analysis, see chap. 7 of Bjork's *Life, Liberty, and Property.*

potentially a very inefficient way to deal with negative spillover effects, which arise when what I decide to do with my property in some way damages the value or usefulness of my neighbor's property. Zoning is inefficient, for instance, when it precludes mixed land use by mutually compatible activities. Zoning is also inefficient if it precludes users of land in a given area striking a deal whereby those persons wanting to use their land in ways that adversely affect their neighbors could pay a negotiated price to cover the nuisance. Suppose, for example, that the owners of a high-tech manufacturing firm want to build a plant on a site that is in a chiefly residential area because this location would vastly reduce their employees' commuting time. The firm's owners might be able to satisfactorily offset the subjective costs of any noise or other nuisance to nearby residents by offering to maintain a community park on the land surrounding the plant. But zoning prevents such deals from being struck—deals that have the potential to leave all parties better off.

Zoning presents problems of equity as well as problems of efficiency. It deprives some landowners of the opportunity to make profits by selling their land to buyers who would put it to more intensive uses, ostensibly because the existing community wants protection from some potentially noxious uses of that land. But the community makes no compensation for the reduced value of the landowners' property when it is zoned for less intensive uses. Thus zoning is a police power not unlike eminent domain but without arrangements to compensate owners for certain values they are forced to forego. The economist Gordon Bjork has aptly called zoning a "blunt instrument"—one which aims at improving the total social value of land by precluding varying degrees of incompatible uses, but which simultaneously wipes out opportunities for increased social welfare because fully compatible or compensated multiple uses are not allowed.[5]

One final problem with zoning is that it further tilts economic forces in favor of urban sprawl and income-segregated neighborhoods and against the continued agricultural use of land near growing cities. This problem is triggered by zoning laws that require minimum lot sizes. Mandated large lot sizes, setbacks, side yards, off-street parking, and so forth increase the demand for land per residence. A typical suburban zoning ordinance, for instance, requires that a house be one-and-a-half times the size of that needed for a townhouse. To this excessive requirement must be added the considerably greater amount of land needed for streets serving suburban residential developments. These same zoning laws also lead to income-segregated neighborhoods, because neighborhoods with large lots make

5. See Bjork, *Life, Liberty, and Property,* p. 68.

housing in those areas unaffordable to lower-income people. Further-more, the premature intensive zoning of some lands at the periphery of cities accounts for certain tracts of good agricultural land being left idle—they are too expensive and too fragmented for farming, yet not ready for development. Finally, some exurban (semi-rural residential) areas have begun to require that houses be built on very generous lots—the mini-mum size ranges from one to twenty acres. This adds to existing demands for converting farmland to residential use.

ARE IMPORTANT FOOD-PRODUCING LANDS BEING IRRETRIEVABLY LOST TO URBAN SPRAWL?

Numerous politicians and scholars argue that good agricultural land in the United States and Canada is being too rapidly overtaken by factories, houses, streets, and parking lots. These critics of current land use point out that the decision to pave over or build upon good cropland is prac-tically irreversible. The value of an acre of urban land with buildings on it can easily be one hundred times as great as its current value in crops.[6] Thus, even if food prices were to skyrocket, it would be economically unfeasible to raze the buildings and reclaim the land for agricultural use. The critics of present trends point out that we have several good reasons to worry about premature and irretrievable conversion of cropland to urban uses. Most of the land in North America best suited to agriculture is already in use (although there are years when the federal government uses incentives to encourage more fallowing of land so as to prevent over-production from unduly lowering farm incomes); rates of productivity gain on that land have been tapering off since the mid-1970s; soils world-wide are rapidly being depleted; and continued growth of the world's population and income will put increasing pressures on the American breadbasket (as well as on all other food-producing resources in the world).

If these critics often share a concern about the facts, they do not all agree about the causes or cures for such a calamity in the making. Indeed, a fair number of experts don't feel any great sense of urgency about the matter. They fully expect that the combination of profitable incentives (produced by rising food prices) and human ingenuity will generate fur-ther productivity gains through new and better food production tech-nologies, thereby preventing global disaster. Of course, many people around the world will continue to starve, but this is a consequence of their

6. See the American Assembly, *The Farm and City: Rivals or Allies?* (Englewood Cliffs, N.J.: Prentice-Hall, 1980), p. 129.

limited ability to buy or produce food, not the result of any immediate constraints on America's food-producing capability. It is extremely difficult to sort through the facts, arguments, and "counter facts" and counterarguments that are presented. Do we have an impending problem or don't we? If we do, why is that the case, and what can be done about it?

In the main, economists predict that if *very* strong cumulative evidence points to a rapid rise in food prices in the next decade (based on widespread expectations of increased food demands, fewer productivity gains, and rapid losses of good cropland to urban use), then land markets will respond accordingly. Farmers or speculators will hold onto the best agricultural land, keeping it out of the hands of urban developers and betting that farm prices and incomes will rise sufficiently in the next ten years to compensate them for the foregone earnings of present development. On the other hand, if food and cropland scarcities are not imminent—if they will occur not in the next ten years but in the next century—then it is not so likely that unencumbered land markets will make the socially "right" decisions about allocations of land between urban and agricultural uses.

There are two reasons why private markets may respond inadequately to possible events in the more distant future. First, there is no way that future generations can directly offer to pay present generations for keeping lands in agricultural use as a form of insurance against the possibility of a disastrous future food shortage. (Moral obligations toward future generations will be dealt with in the next section.) The second reason that markets may not adequately protect against future scarcity has to do with the way that anticipated future returns are capitalized. Taxes are levied on corporate profits and again on the dividends or interest that individuals earn on the monies they invest in business stocks and bonds. As a result, the rate of return that businesses have to get on their ventures must exceed the rate of return that private individuals expect to make on their savings. This discrepancy is a tax "wedge" between the rate at which savers find it acceptable to part with current spending opportunities and the rate that businesses must get on their ventures. One or the other of these two rates (or some average of the two) will be used in calculations capitalizing future returns in land use (or the returns on any other asset). The higher the rate, however, the less attractive are the returns expected in the distant future. Since the higher interest rate will be used in a business assessment of whether it is worthwhile to hold land for its future agricultural value, a strong bias can exist against preserving farmland now as an investment in the distant future. Furthermore, currently high interest rates combined with low crop prices reduce farmers' cash flow, and so diminish their ability to undertake costly steps to preserve soil fertility over time.

These interest-rate problems suggest that exclusive reliance on land markets may not adequately protect food supplies into the distant future. If society becomes concerned about the matter, various remedies are available. Nonagricultural uses of certain lands can be limited by laws (similar to local zoning practices but with a different objective), or development rights to good agricultural land that is "endangered" can be purchased with public monies. Some protection (though not extending into the far-distant future) could also be afforded by changing the current tax system to eliminate the tax wedge between interest rates paid to savers and rates of return earned by corporate investments in new plants and equipment.

Should society intervene (and if so, how extensively) in land and other natural resource markets to slow the rate at which these resources are exploited? The answer depends largely on the degree of optimism that can reasonably be entertained about future technological advances providing substitutes for land and for other essentially nonrenewable resources that supply us with food, energy, and so forth. Obviously, if the prospects of such advances were virtually certain, then slowing down current rates of resource use would mean unnecessarily foregoing some of the output they presently provide. For instance, prospective federal or state land-use plans that call for greenbelt agricultural zoning around urban areas would deny some members of this generation the opportunity to live on that land or to buy products that could be produced more cheaply there than on other sites.

DO WE HAVE OBLIGATIONS TO FUTURE GENERATIONS?

Here we run up against the problems of intergenerational equity. Should we the current generation recognize some sort of obligation to preserve the natural resource base, including agricultural land, for future generations, and do so at some sacrifice to ourselves? It seems perfectly clear that Scripture's teaching about our stewardship over the earth should be interpreted in light of God's desire to sustain and bless each generation with the earth's resources. We are told that the earth does not belong to us but rather to God, and that our human role is to develop these resources and enjoy their fruits, but also to husband them for those who will later "inherit" them.[7]

7. Wesley Granberg-Michaelson has powerfully argued that our responsibility is not only to humans and their needs but also to other members of creation, since redemption also encompasses them. See *A Worldly Spirituality: The Call to Redeem the Earth* (San Francisco: Harper & Row, 1984).

We should bear in mind that Scripture does not neatly separate time into past, present, and future, as we do. What to us is a past sacrifice or future promise is, according to Scripture, a very real claim or blessing upon our present. This implies that our human decisions about land use ought also to have a degree of timelessness about them. The Scripture's teaching bears some resemblance to the belief of Native American peoples that land may be used for present needs but must also be held in trust for the benefit of future human and animal life.

Certain secular ethicists make a similar argument. The best-known to economists is the work of John Rawls, a philosopher at Harvard. His ethical analysis of income distribution can easily be applied to rates of natural resource use. Suppose that all generations ever to be born were to send representatives to a constitutional assembly that would decide how nonrenewable resources should be used.[8] Furthermore, imagine that no representative is actually aware of which generation he or she represents, or what race, social stratum, and so forth he or she will belong to. A constitutional arrangement for allocating resources among people and across time that is likely to receive the delegates' unanimous approval would have two features. First, it would reward people in proportion to their productive efforts, thereby insuring over time the highest standard of living possible, given the initial endowment of resources. Second, income gaps among individuals and generations would be permitted only to the extent that these gaps encouraged productivity advances benefiting the *poorest* members and generations of society. Delegates would not knowingly vote for an arrangement that would permit one generation to live high on the resource "hog" at the expense of later generations. Thus future generations would not be shortchanged.

A logical application of scriptural and Rawlsian principles to intergenerational resource use suggests that each generation should be responsible for undertaking actions that preserve the resource base into the indefinite future. Neither scriptural nor Rawlsian principles would entail an obligation to preserve at all costs a specific resource such as coal, since its increased scarcity serves to prompt important technical progress that provides alternative, renewable sources of energy—a boon not only to this generation but also to succeeding generations. On the other hand, these principles can be used to justify social actions that would slow rates of resource utilization when the costs of a resource *bundle,* compared to prices generally, are found to rise considerably over time. With subsoil

---

8. For this application of Rawls's analysis, see chaps. 8 and 9 of Bjork's *Life, Liberty, and Property.*

resources, for example, reduced utilization could be achieved by charging "severance" taxes on each unit of material being extracted. What such a tax does, of course, is to push up the prices paid by final users of that material and of products manufactured with its help. Higher consumer prices deflect consumer demand toward less expensive substitutes and induce technological innovations making more economical use of the scarcer material.

WHAT ARE THE BEST MEANS AVAILABLE FOR PRESERVING FOOD-PRODUCING LAND?

Both Rawlsian ethics and scriptural teaching appear to call for some efforts to preserve food-producing resources—which now include the sea as well as land, and may one day include resources elsewhere in the solar system. As we've mentioned before, there are essentially two ways that food-producing lands can be protected from premature conversion to urban use. A state or provincial land-use plan might designate certain land for exclusive agricultural use and prohibit its sale for urban development. Alternatively, public tax monies could be used to buy development rights to targeted land that is highly productive in agricultural use but is succumbing to pressures from nearby urban expansion. A third and very important policy necessary to preserving the food resource base is a comprehensive plan to reduce topsoil loss. In principle there are ways that fees could be used to elicit greater efforts from farmers to preserve topsoils.

A number of attempts have been made in Canadian provinces and U.S. states to formulate land-use plans aimed at preserving the best food-producing lands.[9] The devices used have included lower or deferred taxes on farm property, preferential treatment of inheritance and estate taxes for farms (following a similar change in estate taxation by the federal government), purchase of development rights to certain endangered agricultural lands, and mandatory agricultural districting. None of these by themselves are thought to have been highly successful in slowing down the rate at which agricultural land is converted to urban use. Although quite popular with farmers, lower or deferred taxes tend to provide too little inducement to maintain land in farms, since they come nowhere close to bridging the gap between agricultural and urban market values for the lands in question. Furthermore, some of these tax relief programs have been diverted to other than their intended purposes, enabling spec-

9. See Owen J. Furuseth and John T. Pierce, *Agricultural Land in an Urban Society* (Washington: Association of American Geographers, 1982).

ulators to enjoy lower costs while they hold land that will be developed at virtually the same pace at which it would have been developed without the special tax treatment.

The chief disadvantage of trying to control land use through the public purchase of development rights to endangered land is the high cost of these rights. In New Jersey they have ranged from $331 per acre in Burlington County to $3,120 per acre in Suffolk County. Development rights recently purchased in King County, Washington (where Seattle is located), cost $2,723 per acre. On the basis of projections about the total number of acres that are expected to be converted from farm use to urban use by the year 2000, the purchase of development rights to only half the endangered acres at their 1980 cost in King County (a minimum, since prices will rise rapidly above this level before the year 2000 as urban pressures mount) would be $19 billion. This is the equivalent of eighteen percent of what U.S. states and localities spent on public education in 1980. We must look the costliness of such a program squarely in the face, because doing so helps us to evaluate more honestly the sacrifices entailed by a larger commitment to saving farmland from urban encroachment. These costs must be compared with estimates of potential food scarcity in the future before saving farmland can be given a high or low priority for public funding.

Unfortunately, one reason for the popularity of direct public intervention limiting land-use choices—in preference to outright public purchase of development rights—is that direct controls partially conceal the actual economic and ethical costs of altering land-use patterns. Geographers have paid considerable attention to British Columbia's experience with comprehensive land-use planning, which was initiated in the late 1970s. The plan included the establishment of an agricultural land reserve through province-wide zoning of all land that had agricultural potential and that the planners deemed to be unnecessary for urban growth in the next five years. This is exclusive farm-use zoning. Legislation in this province also provides for the creation of greenbelts around cities, the development of urban and industrial land-banks and reserves, and the setting aside of land for recreational use.

British Columbia's system of agricultural land reserves is compulsory but does provide some income protection to farmers who have been deprived of the right to sell their land for higher-valued urban use. Because compensation is less than that which would prevail with the province's purchase of development rights, this approach produces budget savings. However, it does so only at the expense of some coercion and losses to some holders of farmland. Despite these negative aspects, this approach has proved popular in the province. It may be that the equity costs of the reserve program are not extreme, and there may be a sense that the burdens of farmland protection are being fairly shared among taxpayers and farmland owners. Several investigators judge this program to be a success because the rate of land conversion to urban use in British Columbia has slowed in the past several years.

In some U.S. states and counties with districts that employ measures to encourage voluntary, exclusively agricultural land use, the results have been more mixed. In New York state, where this approach has been in place for the longest time, financial incentives appear to have been insufficient to reduce the rate of land conversion to urban use. Obviously, making the approach more effective would mean either spending more money on incentives or making the plans more coercive. The path British Columbia has taken may be a legitimate compromise between the two approaches, but it's hard to evaluate the fairness of the particular way in which their mandatory approach allocates the burdens. If it is in the interest of the general public to preserve farmland, should it not be fully at the expense of their own tax dollars rather than partially by "conscription" of land? Furthermore, it is not clear that state and provincial planners have a broad enough overview of, sufficient expertise about, or great enough influence upon the factors affecting the supply and demand of land for agricultural and other uses to make the best land-use decisions.

It is indicative of British Columbia's necessarily parochial view that the concerns which prompted its foray into widespread planning focused on its desire to be less dependent on food imported from other parts of Canada and other countries (especially the United States and Mexico). However, in the larger national perspective, the types of agricultural land that British Columbian authorities might feel called upon to preserve may be much less important than certain very productive farmlands in other parts of Canada. Actions that could be taken at the federal level to preserve farmland in the United States would benefit from the resources of a centralized administration capable of making long-range estimates concerning population, technology, export policy, land reclamation needs, and other factors affecting food prices and the desirability of preserving farmland. Then, presumably, development rights to good farmland in danger of being lost to urban development could be purchased in such a way that ten acres of highly productive land outside Des Moines, Iowa, could be "saved" for future agricultural needs for the cost of the rights to one acre of such land outside Trenton, New Jersey—thereby providing greater total farmland protection at much less cost than separate state-level plans could achieve. Similarly, we can anticipate that effective international policy coordination and funding may one day enable the world's peoples to make direct comparisons of global costs and benefits before undertaking the preservation of any critical food-producing lands.

SUMMARY AND IMPLICATIONS

Many economists are loath to make ethical judgments. Nonetheless, we have made one such major judgment by supporting the argument that the living owe some special consideration to future generations in the timing and extent of their resource use. With respect to land use, it is clear that a variety of imperfections exist naturally in land markets (the various spillover effects we mentioned earlier) and that current tax policies tilt private decisions in favor of geographically extensive urbanization. Zoning for the purpose of reducing negative spillover effects appears to have cost citizens more—in terms of inefficient land use and ethically arbitrary allocations of the burdens and benefits—than is popularly realized. Many of the concerns about incompatible land uses could be dealt with more directly through private negotiations (perhaps facilitated through public intervention) between the affected parties. Even though the intention is laudable, provincial and state zoning for the purpose of preserving valuable food-producing land into the distant future seems to be an economically and ethically deficient technique being implemented at the wrong level of government.

One way of minimizing the potential for acute future scarcities of food-producing land can be better understood in the light of the analysis presented in this chapter. This approach involves interpreting any significant upward trend in world food prices as a warning of possible future problems. This interpretation of price data is especially appropriate if projected trends in land fertility (which are affected by erosion, fertilizer application, irrigation levels, and rates of improved seed adoption) and conditions in international trade and finance make future output prospects appear bleak. Such circumstances might justify making efforts to redress the artificial bias (due to taxes and public utility prices) now favoring rapid urbanization. If this measure alone were to prove insufficient to significantly reduce the rate at which farmland is lost to urban sprawl, then public (federally financed) acquisition of development rights to "strategic" food-producing resources is a tool that could be tried. The chief virtues of such a tool include the explicit revelation of costs imposed, its voluntary nature, and the sharing of cost burdens among the entire taxable public for the sake of future generations.

Our examination of land-use problems and the possible solutions to them makes us better equipped to engage in enlightened discussions about the use of other resources such as forests, fisheries, and energy supplies. We can see that when the public becomes concerned about *how* resources are being used, it is valuable to devise efficient ways to reduce any unintended negative spillover effects or fiscal incentives that unduly favor one resource use over another. We can also appreciate the very important work that markets do by inducing the most profitable use of a resource. Furthermore, we recognize that debates about possibly improvident rates of resource use will call for our balancing what is known (for example, recent price trends for a cluster of resources) against what is hoped for (such as the development of resource substitutes by funded research projects), while paying due respect to the interests of both present and future generations.

Questions for Further Consideration

1. Do you find yourself optimistic or pessimistic about the potential of technology to provide the world with greater output and rising standards of living? Are those who expect further technological developments to extend the life of or provide substitutes for diminishing resources guilty of misplaced idolatry, or are they simply good analysts?

2. What kind of balance do you want to see among the various views of landed property: the Lockean insistence on unrestricted private ownership as a guarantee of liberty; the utilitarian defense of private property for its social benefits; and the biblical view that land belongs to God but is to be used by stewardly "owners" for both their own needs and those of the community?

3. Do you think that rights of landowners over the use and disposition of their property should be legally regulated in order to remedy the weakness of markets in dealing with positive and negative spillover effects? If so, should Christians favor any one of the following devices over another: zoning and land-use plans, the public purchase of development rights, or changes in tax policy that now favors one use (like sprawling urban development) over another?

4. To what extent do present generations have an obligation to preserve resources into the future? Is this obligation adequately met by the functioning of resource markets? Compare the several quotations at the opening of this chapter.

CHAPTER EIGHT

Trade Policy: The External and Internal Effects of International Interdependence

A FABLE ABOUT PROTECTIONISM

Mr. Manufacturer and Cabinet Minister:

I am a carpenter, as Jesus was; I wield the hatchet and the adze to serve you.

Now, while I was chopping and hewing from dawn to dusk on the states of our lord the king, it occurred to me that my labor is as much a part of our *domestic* industry as yours.

And ever since, I have been unable to see any reason why protection should not come to the aid of my woodyard as well as your factory.

For after all, if you make cloth, I make roofs. We both, in different ways, shelter our customers from the cold and the rain.

Yet I have to run after my customers, whereas yours run after you. You have found a way of forcing them to do so by preventing them from supplying themselves elsewhere [with cheaper foreign goods], while my customers are free to turn to whomever they like. . . .

I do not come to you and demand, as I have a full right to do, that you withdraw the *restriction* you are imposing on your customers; I prefer to follow the prevailing fashion and claim a little *protection* for myself. . . .

I have discovered [a] means of benefiting the sons of St. Joseph; and you will welcome it all the more readily, I hope, as it in no way differs from the means you employed in maintaining the privilege that you vote for yourself every year.

The wonderful means I have in mind consists in forbidding the use of sharp hatchets in France.

I maintain that this *restriction* would be no more illogical or more arbitrary than the one to which you subject us in the case of your cloth.

Why do you drive out the Belgians? Because they undersell you. And why do they undersell you? Because they are in some respect superior to you as textile manufacturers.

Between you and a Belgian, consequently, there is exactly the same difference as between a dull hatchet and a sharp hatchet.

And you are forcing me—me, a carpenter—to buy from you the product of a dull hatchet.

Look upon France as a workman who is trying, by his labor, to obtain everything he needs, including cloth.

There are two possible ways of doing this:

The first is to spin and weave the wool himself.

The second is to produce other commodities—for instance, clocks, wallpaper, or wine—and to exchange them with the Belgians for the cloth.

Of these two procedures the one that gives the better result may be represented by the sharp hatchet; the other is the dull hatchet.

You do not deny that at present, in France, it requires *more labor* to obtain a piece of cloth directly from our looms (the dull hatchet) than indirectly by our vines (the sharp hatchet). You are so far from denying this that it is precisely because of this *additional toil* (which, according to you, is what wealth consists in) that you request, nay more, you *impose,* the use of the poorer of the two hatchets.

Now, at least be consistent; be impartial; and if you mean to be just, give us poor carpenters the same treatment you give yourself.

Enact a law to this effect:

"No one shall use beams or joists save those produced by dull hatchets."
Consider what the immediate effect will be.

Where we now strike a hundred blows with the hatchet, we shall then strike three hundred. What we now do in one hour will take three hours. What a mighty stimulus to employment! Apprentices, journeymen, and masters, there will no longer be enough of us. We shall be in demand, and therefore well paid. Whoever wants to have a roof made will be henceforth obliged to accept our demands, just as whoever wants cloth today is obliged to submit to yours.

Claude-Frédéric Bastiat, "The Two Hatchets"

The international exchange of goods, services, money, and people has for centuries raised questions of fairness in the minds of both participants and observers. Is trade a thinly disguised form of exploitation in which rich nations become better off at the expense of poorer nations? Both the fear of exploitation and popular fears of the dislocations caused by vigorous foreign competition have prompted all nations to tax, limit, and even prohibit the import of foreign goods, money, and people in varying degrees. In these times, "saving U.S. jobs" from foreign competition in the steel and automobile industries has become a key feature of congressional and presidential debates, and the subject of difficult discussions among world leaders. Unfortunately, the costs of ceding to pressures for trade restrictions are usually ignored, both because they are somewhat hidden from view and because the benefits of relatively free trade are not widely appreciated. Yet trade is an important material expression of our human interdependence—one that deserves the thoughtful consideration that Christians usually give to their charitable offerings.

Discussion of the "how" question, which was addressed in Chapter Three, focused on a firm's choice of production inputs—for instance, about whether to use coal or oil as fuel, glass or aluminum for containers, pesticides or "natural" means for insect control, and so forth. Another type of "how" question is whether to produce a needed input internally or to purchase it from a supplying firm. This latter question would have been irrelevant to Robinson Crusoe even after Friday's arrival. Obviously, whatever they required they would make themselves. Markets, however, afford people an opportunity to choose whether to be self-sufficient or to meet their perceived needs through exchange.

Of course, markets begin to exist only when several people are willing and able to produce surpluses of some things and to exchange these with each other. Such exchanges can be as rudimentary as barter between two parties who dicker over the rate at which shoes will be exchanged for wheat. Much more complex are the types of market exchanges that we described earlier, where would-be suppliers and would-be consumers exchange at a competitive price quoted in money. In many such cases, dickering is out of the question, since neither an individual seller nor an individual buyer is significant enough to affect the price at which the exchange takes place. Buyer and seller may never meet in person; they may be thousands of miles apart. They may share very few values; indeed, their nations may even regard each other as enemies. Nevertheless, what draws the two parties into the exchange is the opportunity to mutually benefit from the trade.

For the sake of clarity, we will use the term "trade" to designate interchanges of goods and services across borders, and the term "exchange" to designate domestic interchanges. However, most of the moral and economic issues involved in trade are not much different from those arising out of exchanges taking place within a single nation: What's a fair price? Who's getting the best deal? Is one person or nation being exploited by another? Consequently, we will first try to understand exchange and the moral issues that have surrounded it before examining international trade. Although in the 1980s these moral issues are raised less often with respect to domestic exchanges, they still loom large in discussions about policies affecting international trade.

CHANGING ATTITUDES TOWARD EXCHANGE AND TRADE: FROM EARLY SKEPTICS TO ADAM SMITH

For many centuries, commercial exchange was viewed with great moral skepticism. Some biblical passages suggest that an honest merchant is hard to find (see Ecclus. 26:29–27:2) and that the wealth of merchants is all too often ill-gotten (see Ezek. 22:12; Hos. 12:7; and Rev. 18:3). Aristotle also had serious reservations about commercial exchange. He recognized that such interchanges enabled people to make their goal wealth-getting instead of simply meeting their subsistence needs. The goal of wealth could corrupt men and women, making them continually strive for more without receiving ultimate satisfaction from their material successes. Aristotle's ideas about commercial exchange and fair pricing and his condemnation of lending at interest had a profound effect on the teaching of Saint Thomas Aquinas and on medieval church law regarding exchange, pricing, and usury.

Some people might suspect that the gradual acceptance of lending at interest and the waning importance of "just price" laws in the Western world were symptomatic of societies grown increasingly secular and of their lesser concern for obedience to biblical and church teaching in everyday life. However, the fact that people gradually agonized less over the morality of most prices and that the paying and receiving of interest finally became acceptable, is better explained by the development of vigorous markets for goods (and for money) since the late Middle Ages. As we've said before, in markets where there are numerous sellers and buyers of each good or service, the "going price" is no longer independently "set" by any single seller or buyer. And the morality of prices becomes less of a concern when the price is arrived at by competitive bidding among many parties rather than by dickering between two isolated individuals.

Furthermore, in the late Middle Ages scholars began to analyze what happens when two people exchange goods or services—analysis that was more definitive by the nineteenth century. Part of the great moral concern over commercial exchange had been that one person was thought to gain at another's expense. Medieval church law on the "just price" was meant to set limits on how much gain one party could in good conscience be allowed. Could sellers legitimately charge prices that exceeded the material and labor costs that went into making their goods? Could they take advantage of extreme need or ignorance on the part of buyers?

On closer examination, it eventually became clear that *both* parties involved in a strictly voluntary exchange must be gaining something. Otherwise, why would they agree to the exchange? The buyer must be gaining, because he or she is giving up money that could have been used to produce the same good or service (or some close substitute) or to purchase it from another supplier. The seller must also be benefiting from the exchange, since alternative outlets usually exist—other buyers or personal use. Historically, as market competition became more vigorous and as the economic pie began to grow due to increasing productivity, it became even clearer to most participants in voluntary exchanges that everyone is better off (evaluated in terms of their own preferences) as a result of exchange. One party is not gaining by exploiting another; both parties are profiting.

Western peoples began to accept market exchange as inevitable, beneficial, and possibly morally justifiable. However, it wasn't until the late 1700s, when Adam Smith, the great father of economics, published his *Wealth of Nations,* that someone vigorously defended and advocated the expansion of market exchange both domestically and internationally. Smith brilliantly observed that where the prospects of exchange grow, production increases and the standard of living rises. The key to this cause and effect? Where more potential customers and producers can be added to a market, it becomes possible for people to increasingly specialize in doing what they do best.

When a market is small, people must perform a diversity of tasks to supply their own needs, and possibly produce a bit of surplus to sell to others. But when a market becomes much larger, it can support the doing of highly specialized tasks. People can devote most of their working time and creativity to one task—like giving violin lessons, designing irrigation equipment, welding airplane parts, and so forth—while depending on the market to sell them food, clothing, shelter, training, and entertainment. Smith claimed that such specialization often enables people to put their minds to devising innovative (i.e., faster and cheaper) ways to produce a product or service. A larger market is also more competitive, which further stimulates innovation, since survival in the marketplace depends on it.

Adam Smith provided marvelous historical examples of how specialization and exchange had greatly enhanced output. He also focused on saving and on the reinvestment of profits for expanding output and raising productivity—both powerful engines of economic growth. He railed against all sorts of remnants of medieval meddling with markets that set prices, restricted the movement of capital and labor, and controlled production. Smith contended that such interference with supply and demand limited market size and consequently reduced the growth of productivity on which higher living standards depend. (If this sounds familiar, it is. The recently popular arguments for "supply-side" economics—which call for lower taxes and less regulation—while often doctrinaire, do borrow some important ideas from classical economic thought.)

Smith's concepts proved to be very important in the ultimate dismantling of restrictions on English domestic exchanges. His ideas about domestic exchange were also logically extended to international trade. Obviously, if growing markets in national trade stimulated production, encouraged innovation, and raised living standards, then growing markets in international trade should do the same. This was a truly revolutionary idea. Before Smith, mercantilism reigned almost without opposition. Mercantilists regarded trade as a political instrument to aggrandize the nation, particularly its sovereign. The emphasis was on using all sorts of devices to promote exports but to discourage imports, since a strongly positive balance of trade would bring gold (the international money of the era) into the country. Gold reserves were considered important largely for military reasons, since they enabled the country to provision an army when fighting a foreign war. But there were other reasons to seek a trade surplus, including the hope to thereby maintain high levels of home employment.

Smith logically argued that if trade is good for production and income, then interfering with trade—paying subsidies to exporters, establishing wage controls to keep export prices competitive, imposing tariffs and other restrictions against imports—is a sure way to achieve economic stagnation. After all, when a country attempts to protect itself from imports and promote exports, it chooses to ignore four fundamental principles.

First, it rarely makes sense to produce something for yourself if someone else is willing to sell you the same quantity and quality at a lower cost. The fact that the seller is a foreigner should in most cases not interfere with this logic.

Second, because resources are scarce, it is unwise to officially promote exports by selling them at subsidized prices to foreigners. Doing so robs other economic sectors of the resources that profitable market prices indicate are more valuable in production for domestic use than for export. (Profitability, as we recall from Chapter Three, is the market's way of conveying information about the relative importance of different wants and a measure of relative efficiencies in different productive sectors.)

Third, suppressing imports and promoting exports in an effort to achieve a favorable balance of trade produces an inflow of foreign currencies whose value to consumers is nil. In fact, a nation able to run a continual trade deficit (as the United States has done since the mid-1970s) benefits by foreigners' willingness to sell that nation goods while simply holding their currency (such as dollars) in its official monetary reserves. Those reserves held by foreign countries in fact do them little good, except for the interest they earn. (This logic also implies that the United States, while running a trade deficit that is in part due to import restrictions in Japan, can actually benefit from Japan's willingness to accept payment in dollars for her exports to America rather than using those dollars to buy American goods. After all, producing dollars for Japan to hold uses up virtually none of the scarce resources that would be needed to produce real goods for export.)

Fourth, the logical inadequacy of national policies to create an excess of exports over imports (a trade surplus) is obvious when one realizes that *all* nations cannot simultaneously have export surpluses. All exchanges require that there be buyers as well as sellers. The revenues generated by sales to some customers are recycled to purchase goods and services from the same or other trading partners.

PROTECTIONIST PLEAS OF UNFAIR COMPETITION VS. OPPORTUNITIES FOR MUTUAL GAIN

Smith's arguments in favor of free domestic exchange and free international trade eventually prompted important policy changes in England and in continental Europe during the nineteenth century. Nonetheless, worries about unfair competition from foreign nations fired lively parliamentary and public debates, just as they do today. Claude-Frédéric Bastiat, the famous French economic satirist whose fable about protectionism begins this chapter, used biting wit to defend free trade against the charge of "unfair competition." His best-known work is a short satiric parable in which candlemakers petition parliament to grant them relief from an unfair foreign competitor. This competitor is accused of flooding the French market with light that does not depend on candles. He offers light at no cost—clearly unfair competition to the candlemakers, who must cover their expenses for materials and wages! The competitor is ultimately identified as none other than the sun, and parliament is asked to require that all French homes be shuttered up. The candlemakers argue that this law would increase the demand for artificial light, and thus would save the jobs of candlemakers as well as promote jobs for many others in the community—including shepherds and olive growers, who supply the candlemakers with the tallow and oil they need.

The argument for protection against unfair competition is still very much with us in the 1980s. It is the clarion call of U.S. automakers, steel producers, textile manufacturers, sugar-beet farmers, pharmaceutical suppliers, and many others. They and their workers raise a cry of "unfair competition" whenever foreign firms make inroads into domestic markets by offering goods at lower prices than those of domestic producers. We are told that such competition is "unfair" because the wages of Indian textile workers are lower, because the Japanese government subsidizes export industries like automobile manufacturing, because foreign steel producers sell below "full cost" in the U.S. market, because European pharmaceutical firms are not burdened by restrictive testing requirements, and because sugar cane is too cheap a source of sugar (compared with sugar beets). We are told that protection of certain domestic producers would also strengthen the entire economy by supporting the jobs of those who supply these protected industries, an argument identical to that of Bastiat's candlemakers.

Even if all these complaints were valid, should they make any difference to us? Are they reasonable arguments for departing from a regime of free trade? The most disturbing observation one can make about claims of "unfair competition" is that they have no natural limit. They can be and are made by producers in dozens of U.S. industries: by large, highly capital-intensive industries like steel manufacturers; by labor-intensive industries in which firms are small, like the shoe and textile industries; and even by "higher-tech" industries like chemical producers. These claims also have their flip-side counterparts in other countries. American producers might worry that "cheap labor" in India makes Indian textile exports to the United States jeopardize American jobs. But in India there are cries for tariff protection from unfair competition based on "cheap capital," which makes American exports endanger Indian jobs! If the governments of all trading nations were to consistently heed the endless cries for protection, the flow of world trade would dwindle to a small trickle. With the collapse of trade, the standard of living now enjoyed by rich nations like our own would fall drastically, while poor nations' hopes for trade-stimulated growth would be dashed.

It is precisely this sequence of trade collapse and plummeting incomes that the world witnessed during the Great Depression. Recessions always rekindle latent demands for job protection in the form of tariffs, bans, or quotas against foreign products. These are appropriately called "beggar-thy-neighbor" policies, since they attempt to shift the burden of unemployment onto workers in foreign lands. Unfortunately, when all nations respond accordingly, drastic reductions in export demand everywhere cause a cumulative decline in national incomes and employment. The Smoot-Hawley Bill of 1930, which severely restricted U.S. imports, was quickly matched by similar measures elsewhere. As a result, world trade in the 1930s shrank to a fraction of its level in the 1920s.[1] This made the worldwide depression much more severe and long-lasting than it need have been. So, while protecting jobs with tariffs may appear to be a

1. See Barry W. Poulson, *Economic History of the United States* (New York: Macmillan, 1981), p. 508.

valuable temporary expedient, it is in fact an extremely dangerous path to follow.

From time to time, the claim of unfair competition is used to kindle a more general fear about a nation's ability to compete in any of the world's markets. If U.S. steel and automobile industries—once the envy of the world—are unable to compete, what hope is there for U.S. export capability in the future? Relatively poor nations fear that because their workers are unskilled, they lack modern technology, and capital is very scarce, they will not be able to find a niche in *any* world market. Is it indeed likely that some nations—the United States or Bangladesh—will simply find themselves out of the world export market altogether?

This very question was addressed in the early nineteenth century by David Ricardo, an Englishman who was an immediate intellectual descendant of Adam Smith. Using a simple example involving two nations and two goods, he was able to show that nations will find it to their advantage to trade whenever their endowments of human and natural resources differ or whenever the tastes of their populations are not identical.

Let's briefly explore an instance in which two countries—say, the United States and India—have similar tastes but different endowments and capabilities. The United States can produce corn more economically than fabric, and India can produce fabric more economically than corn. Nevertheless, U.S. productivity outstrips that of India in both corn and fabric. Per labor hour, the United States can produce, let's say, twenty bushels of corn for every ten bushels India can produce, and fifteen yards of fabric for every twelve yards India can produce.

According to these hypothetical numbers, it might seem that these nations would have no reason to trade. But notice that while the United States is one hundred percent more productive than India in producing corn, it is only twenty-five percent more productive in producing fabric. Thus it will prove to be an advantage for the United States to specialize in producing corn (where it is said to have a "comparative advantage") and trade its corn for fabric from India. Why? Well, by releasing one unit of labor from fabric production, the United States is able to increase corn production by twenty bushels, with which it can then buy approximately twenty yards of fabric (assuming a rate of exchange, or price, of one bushel of corn for one yard of fabric). The net gain is five more yards of cloth than "home production" would supply (at the rate of fifteen yards per unit of labor). India, on the other hand, can release one unit of labor from corn production, which will enable it to boost fabric output by twelve yards. These twelve yards can then be traded for twelve bushels of corn (again, at the price of one bushel for one yard). Thus, for the same labor expended, India enhances its standard of living by two bushels of corn over what it was when India was self-sufficient in both fabric and corn.

The above example illustrates Ricardo's strongest argument in favor of international trade—namely, that countries are able to devote their respective resources to producing what they produce at relatively less cost than another nation, and then trade for the goods or services they produce at relatively greater cost. Both trading nations can thereby enjoy a level of consumption that exceeds that which their domestic production capabilities alone could provide. Amazingly, this holds true even when one nation can boast greater productivity in both goods—as the example above illustrates. In fact, this example is exactly the argument that Adam Smith was making (in words rather than numbers) for the advantages of both domestic market exchange and international trade. In both cases, specialization and exchange promote higher living standards in the form of more food, clothing, and other items.

THE PROBLEM OF "EXPLOITATION"

Even if trade results in mutual benefits, it will not always be equally advantageous to both parties. The terms (or prices) at which an exchange takes place reflect the relative bargaining strength of each party. "Exploitation," a term often applied without great precision, is sometimes used to describe the situation of a poor country's selling its products at prices not terribly favorable to itself but highly advantageous to the industrialized countries buying from it. This can happen if the poor country is selling in a highly competitive world product market where the price charged is really beyond the country's control because it is subject to worldwide supply-and-demand conditions. A low selling price for a certain product can also result from a multinational corporation's operating within a less developed country and maintaining monopolized control over a key resource. (This is especially true if there are not other firms in the country competing vigorously for the labor and other production resources required by the multinational corporation.)

It is sometimes assumed that the answer to exploitation (in which one country has by far the greater advantage in trade than another) can be remedied by a concerned public's haranguing multinational corporations about their moral responsibilities to pay "fair" prices (or "fair" wages to local workers), or even by national governments' expropriating the properties of multinational corporations. Unfortunately, the problem of highly unequal advantage in trade is not amenable to such simple solutions. Countries that fail to enjoy significant gains from trade in their traditional export markets simply do not have the economic leverage to dictate or even cajole buyers into paying higher prices for their products. In some rare cases (petroleum is one example), less developed countries have been able to create cartels for their key exports, which enable them to charge higher prices by restricting supplies to the world market. However, these cartels often break down due to political and economic differences among producing nations (as is happening in OPEC in the mid-1980s). Consequently, the most promising remedy for unequal advantage in trade is general economic development (the subject of Chapter Five). Development entails rising productivity (including the export sector) and increasing economic diversification, which together enable a poor country to gain more from trade by selling a greater volume and variety of products in high demand.

THE SHORT- AND LONG-RUN COSTS OF EVER-POPULAR PROTECTIONISM

With respect to industry arguments for protection from unfair competition, the world has not changed much since the time of Ricardo and Bastiat. When an industry like the steel industry in the United States pleads for special treatment to protect itself from the buffeting of foreign competition, politicians listen. If the plight of the owners does not persuade them, the anguish of unemployed workers in the industry often will. No one should minimize the power or the significance of these pleas for help. However, the trouble with the argument for protection is that it is based on a parochial view, limited to the interests of one industry. It is based on the costs of competition faced by that industry, not on the economy-wide benefits enjoyed when trade is free.

The most convincing argument for the wisdom of resisting protectionist pressures is a thorough inventory of the costs generated by protectionism. If the overriding purpose of devices used for the protection of domestic markets is to save certain jobs, who pays for this job safety net, and how much? Can the benefits—however humane they may appear—possibly outweigh the costs?

Protectionism can take several forms: outright quantitative restrictions on foreign imports (quotas); special taxes added to the prices of foreign imports (tariffs); requirements that only American goods or services be purchased with public tax monies; and import restrictions ostensibly based on health or environmental concerns. For that matter, the so-called "voluntary" restrictions on exports to the United States that are some-

TABLE 1
COSTS OF TARIFFS, BY PRODUCT CATEGORY

Product	Annual cost to U.S. consumers (millions of 1980 dollars)	Source	Year of estimate
Selected agricultural	317	a	1980
Aluminum	286	b	1980
Chemicals	829	b	1980
Copper	1,589	c	1979
Flatware (stainless steel)	31	c	1979
Footwear	1,037	b	1980
(Footwear, nonrubber)	(14)	d	(1977)
Furniture and fixtures	926	b	1980
Glass and glass products	906	b	1980
Jewelry	83	a	1980
Leather products	183	b	1980
Iron and steel	4,047	b	1980
Machinery (electric)	5,646	b	1980
Machinery (nonelectric)	5,324	b	1980
Metal products	386	b	1980
Miscellaneous manufacturing	1,005	b	1980
Paper, paper products	129	b	1980
Printing and publishing	466	b	1980
CB transceivers	57	d	1977
Sugar	1,742	d	1977
Textiles	3,160	b	1980
Transport equipment	4,955	b	1980
Wearing apparel	11,795	b	1980
Wood, wood products	710	b	1980
Zinc	175	c	1979
Total cost of tariffs listed	45,784		

[a]International Trade Commission, statistical services.

[b]Author's estimate.

[c]Charles Pearson, "Adjusting to Imports of Manufacturers from Developing Countries," in *The International Economy: U.S. Role in a World Market*, prepared for the Joint Economics Committee of Congress, December, 1980.

[d]Morris E. Morkre and David G. Tarr, *Effects of Restrictions on United States Imports: Five Case Studies and Theory*. Federal Trade Commission, Bureau of Economics, June 1980.

times negotiated with foreign governments are also forms of protectionism. They are all indirect taxes on American consumers and on the producers of unprotected products. They have the effect of deflecting demand away from foreign imports, thereby causing the prices of domestic goods to rise.

TABLE 2
ESTIMATES OF ANNUAL COSTS TO CONSUMERS PER JOB PROTECTED

Product	Category of re-straint	Average compensa-tion (mil-lions of 1980 dol-lars)	Subsidy from consumer per job (millions of 1980 dollars)	Ratio of subsidy to actual compensa-tion	Source
Television	Tariffs, quotas	12,923	74,155	5.7	a
Footwear	Tariffs, quotas	8,340	77,714	9.3	b
Carbon steel	Tariffs, quotas	24,329	85,272	3.5	a
Steel	TPM	24,329	110,000	4.5	c
Autos	Domestic content bill (pro-posed)	23,566	85,400	3.6	d

*Average annual total compensation comes from the average yearly wages in the U.S. Department of Labor's Labor Force Statistics Derived From the *Current Population Survey: A Databook* (Volume I), September 1982, p. 534, adjusted to allow for fringe benefits in total compensation. The figure used for fringe benefits was 23%, as reported in the *Statistical Abstract of the United States*, p. 400, Table 644.

aCrandall, op. cit.
bInternational Trade Commission, TA-201-19.
cCrandall, "Steel Imports: Dumping or Competition?" *Regulation*, July/August 1980.
dCouncil of Economic Advisers.

The dollar amount by which trade restrictions raise prices has been estimated for a number of American products by Michael Munger; Tables 1 and 2 appeared in a piece he wrote entitled "The Costs of Protectionism: Estimates of the Hidden Tax of Trade Restraint."[2] The phenomenal total cost is forty-six billion dollars for tariffs, and twelve billion dollars for quantitative restrictions. Together, these costs equal the value of *all* U.S. imports of machinery and manufactured goods, or 2.2 percent of the GNP in 1980. This amounts to an annual tax of more than $1,000 on an average family of four. The costs per job saved by tariff and quota protection are listed by industry in Table 2—ranging from $78,000 for the shoe indus-

2. Munger's piece is Chapter Four in *World and Trade Finance* (Albany: Matthew Bender, 1985).

try to $110,000 for the steel industry. The cost of import restrictions runs three to nine times the annual wages of workers who are kept employed in these industries! The conclusion should be obvious: import restrictions are a *very* expensive way to save certain jobs, involuntarily financed by consumers' paying higher prices.

Furthermore, import restrictions typically raise the cost of those items most important in the budgets of poor American families. This means that the high-wage jobs of steelworkers are saved at the expense of lower-income consumers. Taking another example, U.S. trade restrictions on clothing, sugar, and car imports alone were estimated to raise the 1984 tax liability of poor American households by 66 percent. This "tax surcharge" on poor families had seven times the impact that the same import restrictions had on the tax liability of high-income households![3]

It is a terrible waste of scarce economic resources to save a job at a cost equal to nine times the salary being earned by the worker. Happily, alternatives to trade restrictions do exist—alternatives that focus on assisting workers whose jobs disappear because of foreign competition. Existing legislation already provides for "adjustment assistance payments" in cases where widespread job losses can be traced to higher levels of foreign imports. Unfortunately, the way in which this assistance has been administered to date discourages worker relocation to other work sectors and geographical regions. Consequently, while this approach does provide some cushion for worker incomes, it does so at great cost to economic efficiency.

A well-designed adjustment assistance program should encourage worker relocation and/or retraining for other jobs by making assistance partially contingent upon workers taking such steps. This is important because long-run competitive success requires that human and financial resources move out of areas where foreign firms are most efficient and into areas where domestic firms have a growing competitive edge. (As a matter of equity, assistance for displaced *older* workers might be made less contingent on their relocation and retraining, since these changes do not enhance reemployment prospects for older workers as much as they do for younger workers.)

Adjustment assistance is a much less costly way than tariffs to handle the economic dislocation caused by foreign competition. Such payments are also just, since they redistribute some of the free trade benefits reaped by consumers to those hardest hit by the inevitable changes. Finally,

---

3. See Susan Hickok, "The Consumer Cost of U.S. Trade Restrictions," *Federal Reserve Bank of New York Quarterly Review*, Summer 1985, pp. 1-12.

these payments are crucial to winning the political battle against protectionism because a partial but effective income cushion for displaced workers would remove some of labor's motivation for joining employers in their cry of "unfair competition."

Comparing the cost of protectionism with the value of jobs saved in the protected industry reveals that protectionism adds up to a very bad "deal." Looked at from the standpoint of overall employment levels, protectionism is even more costly. It is worth remembering that when trade restrictions save jobs in some industries, they automatically jeopardize the jobs of others who work in export sectors. Why? Because potential foreign customers for U.S. products have fewer dollars (earned through their sales in the United States) with which to purchase products and services exported by the United States. Those who raise the cry of protectionism on the basis of saving jobs are always careful to conceal from public debate the fact that jobs saved in one sector take jobs away from workers in other sectors. They are like Bastiat's petitioning candlemakers, who conveniently ignored the jobs that would be lost in other sectors if householders were forced to spend an increasing share of their budgets on candles.

Protectionism means that consumers pay higher prices and workers in export industries lose jobs. And yet another group bears the cost of protectionism: producers in unprotected industries. Their production costs are higher due to competition from protected industries for the same human, physical, and financial resources that they require. Producers who use the products of protected industries (like the steel industry) also find their costs of production are higher than they would otherwise be. Predictably, protection of input industries sometimes leads to increasing pleas for the protection of user industries as well—as the recent history of the U.S. auto industry proves.

Earlier, when discussing the Great Depression, we noted that using trade barriers to protect high employment is risky, because the prospects of international retaliation are great and can provoke a downward spiral in worldwide trade, income, and employment. To this risk we have added the direct costs that protectionism imposes on various domestic groups. Now something must be said about the long-term costs of protectionism. These are difficult to quantify but very important.

Producers who request tariffs, quotas, or other restrictions on their foreign competitors often insist that the home industry needs this respite from market pressures in order to make needed changes in technology, equipment, and so forth—changes expected to improve the industry's productivity. But industries perpetually shielded from competition are notoriously poor innovators. Indeed, the history of poor industrial progress achieved behind protective barriers and of pleas to prolong "temporary" protection (e.g., by the U.S. steel industry) should make us wary of protectionist pleas. Furthermore, one of the beauties of a market system is that if proposed changes to enhance productivity are truly warranted by expected future market conditions, then industries should be able to acquire the necessary funding for these changes through the ordinary channels of financial markets. Substantial prospects of profits attract financial capital like honey draws bees. Generally speaking, there should be no need to create special market protection in order for industries to attract capital needed for productivity improvements.

The argument in favor of trade free of artificial barriers has been advanced by generations of economists. Adam Smith warned of the economic distortions and slower growth prospects caused by government interventions in markets, which have the effect of coaxing or forcing capital into channels where it is less productive. Smith cited interference as the reason why economic progress in England's agricultural sector had been slower than in its budding industrial sector. The antigrowth effects of market interference also accounted for Smith's opposing exclusive English controls of sea trade, strictures which eventually led American colonists to declare their independence. Yet, despite the logic of such reasoning, pleas for protectionism have persisted. Apparently the lesson that trade restrictions slow down advances in productivity and thereby retard economic growth is one that needs to be rearticulated with each generation.

Economists recognize only one major and truly defensible exception to the free trade rule—namely, "infant industries." An infant industry is usually a new industry in a developing country (certainly not the U.S. steel industry in the 1980s), an industry that might be developed and eventually become a successful competitor in domestic and even foreign markets. However, during its "infancy" the industry may not yet be efficient enough to survive in a market flooded by cheap foreign imports. Developing countries have used this argument to justify tariff protection of infant textile industries and other fledgling enterprises. (It is interesting to note that wars—the American Revolutionary War, for example—have isolated domestic producers long enough for some new industries to mature into successful competitors in world markets.)

In the 1950s and 1960s, many Latin American nations used a type of infant-industry logic to justify their emphasis on substituting tariff-protected domestic products for foreign imports. As a consequence, tariffs became part of pervasive price distortions that jeopardized agricultural development, employment, and overall economic efficiency in the region. Understandably, this growth strategy produced fairly widespread disappointment. Perhaps it serves as a lesson, showing that even "respectable" reasons for protectionism can often backfire terribly.

INITIATIVES TOWARD FREER TRADE

Flows of goods, people, and money across borders are much more significant in the 1980s than ever before. In the last decade, for instance, the share of trade in the U.S. GNP more than doubled. By 1978, exports represented 8 percent of the U.S. GNP, and 20-30 percent of the GNP for France, Germany, and the United Kingdom.[4] At one time, economic policymakers in the United States could make decisions about tax and spending almost exclusively on the basis of domestic inflation, employment, and other considerations. Obviously, this isolationist perspective is no longer possible today—when one out of every six jobs in U.S. manufacturing depends on exports, when two out of five acres farmed in America produce crops for export, when one third of U.S. corporate profits are derived from foreign sales and investments,[5] and when one in six dollars used to finance plant expansion and equipment purchases in the United States comes from foreigners.[6]

Independently pursued policies of national taxation, spending, trade, and finance do not make sense in the highly interdependent world of the 1980s; certain types and levels of coordination among nations do. In Chapter Five we explored the mutual interdependence of industrialized and developing nations. Such interdependence means, among other things, that supplying aid to poor developing nations is not solely a matter of justice but also a prudent investment in the present health and continued growth of our own economy.

Neighboring countries are affected by one another's economic health, and this is even more dramatically true of the industrialized market economies currently dependent upon each other through trade and the flow of financial resources. When industrialized market economies are growing at more than 1.5 to 2.0 percent per year, their imports grow at three times this pace. This rate of growth in trade in turn supports and stimulates further growth in real production and buying power. This relationship

---

4. See U.S. Bureau of the Census, *Statistical Abstract of the United States: 1981*, 102d ed. (Washington: U.S. Government Printing Office), p. 876.

5. See C. Fred Bergsten, "Can We Prevent a World Crisis?" *Challenge: The Magazine of Economic Affairs* 25 (Jan.-Feb. 1983): 17-26.

6. *Statistical Abstract of the United States: 1981*, pp. 834, 421.

between trade and incomes is appropriately nicknamed the "virtuous cycle." On the other hand, when these same economies grow at an annual rate of less than 1.5 percent, trade levels fall by a multiple of the shortfall in growth, thereby causing growth itself to slow down or stall completely. Of course, a negative spiral of this sort generates rising pressures for protectionism which, if generalized, simply accelerate economic contraction in the economies of trading partners.

The first line of defense against a debilitating downward spiral of trade, production, and incomes is clear: nations must take further steps to liberalize trade. Experts generally agree that when trade barriers are not in the process of being affirmatively lowered, the slightest economic recession rekindles protectionist pleas. Recently, for instance, the Reagan administration—ideologically committed to free trade—bowed to pressures that restricted trade in cars, textiles, sugar, and steel.

During the 1984 congressional and presidential elections, candidates were openly debating the need for "reciprocity" in trade dealings with Japan and the possibility of "local content" legislation that would cover all sales of cars in the United States.[7] Both of these changes would be a definite step backward for U.S. trade policy and a real danger sign, because until now the United States has been the nation most responsible for leading the world toward freer and much expanded trade. To some extent these measures were proposed to put pressure on the Japanese government to accept "voluntary" trade restrictions on their nation's exports to the United States. Unfortunately, these are actually no less damaging to both economies than unilaterally imposed restrictions. The recent high-level public debate about such nationalist "solutions" to trade problems is a vivid example of the way in which strong protectionist sentiments often capture and exploit public attention, especially during recessions.

INTEREST RATES, THE TRADE BALANCE, AND THE STRENGTH OF THE DOLLAR

International interdependence is also apparent in the flows of financial capital among nations. Together with the flows of goods and services traded, financial flows affect rates of exchange between currencies and vice versa. In 1984, Americans were very concerned about the high level of interest rates. The principal fear was that such high rates would put a damper on spending and thereby blight the possibility of a full recovery from the long recession that was just ending. The high interest rates were

7. Bergsten, "Can We Prevent a World Crisis?" p. 20.

blamed on a very high federal-budget deficit. Its funding out of the same pool of dollars available to the private sector left fewer and more expensive dollars available for investment. These same high interest rates were also affecting international flows of money and goods. High interest rates attracted an inflow of funds from other countries, strengthening the international value of the dollar and making U.S. export prices very uncompetitive in world markets. Many U.S. industries were concerned about lower export earnings, and the outflow of potential investment funds from other countries made them fear a weaker economic recovery.

This recent scenario is a valuable reminder that the relatively easy flow of goods and money among nations today makes economies of all the nations extremely sensitive to the policy choices made in each country. This is true, for instance, with respect to federal budget deficits. In order to grasp the complexity and pervasiveness of this interdependence, we will look briefly at how currency values are determined, what effect they have on the balance of trade, and what temptations exist for governments to tamper with these rates for reasons of purely national interest.

Since the early 1970s, the rates of exchange among British pounds, German marks, U.S. dollars, and other major currencies have been allowed to a large extent to seek their own level in what is referred to as a "float." This means that when U.S. residents have a relatively high demand for foreign currencies—in order to buy foreign goods or to invest in overseas financial markets—the value of those currencies rises vis-à-vis the U.S. dollar (meaning a weaker dollar). When the value of the U.S. dollar falls relative to that of other currencies, an important, natural equilibrating mechanism is activated: the dollar prices of foreign goods rise, thereby reducing U.S. import levels, while the prices of American goods in terms of foreign currencies fall, causing U.S. export levels to rise. Falling import levels and rising export levels constitute an improved balance of trade for the United States.

This is the way things work if national governments do not interfere with the markets for their currencies by "managing the float," and if they do not pursue contradictory fiscal and monetary policies. Why manage a float? The instance above can serve as an example. Under such circumstances, U.S. authorities may believe that the dollar is at an artificially low value relative to one or more foreign currencies. This is a possible concern if, for instance, a declining dollar and rising import prices are creating inflationary pressures at home. The authorities might then try to purchase dollars by selling some of their foreign currency holdings, thereby putting some upward pressure on the value of the U.S. dollar. On the other side of the Atlantic, Common Market countries may also believe the dollar to be undervalued—a concern to them if their export sectors are suffering a decline in sales to the U.S. market. Believing this, they will also buy dollars with their own currencies, thereby raising the dollar's value to a more acceptable level vis-à-vis their own currencies. In this case, a shared view about the undervaluation of the dollar would lead to mutually complementary float interventions on both sides of the Atlantic.

Unfortunately, disagreement about the long-run equilibrium rate of exchange between two currencies (reflecting underlying competitive conditions, which are affected by different national rates of productivity growth or inflation) is rather common. Consequently, if governments intervene in the float, they will often do so at cross-purposes. In the above instance, for example, the United States might not have any complaints about the dollar's value, especially since a relatively weak dollar causes U.S. export sales to improve and U.S. employment to rise. Together these factors produce important political advantages for the administration in office. Nonetheless, the Common Market countries may *not* agree that the dollar is appropriately priced (especially when their export industries are being hurt by a strong mark or franc). Their intervention in exchange markets to raise the dollar's value relative to that of their own currencies would run counter to U.S. interests. What we have in float manipulation is something not unlike the active nationalist use of tariffs and quotas to manipulate trade flows in favor of a given country.

No nation unilaterally can hope forever to tamper with exchange rates. Using exchange rate manipulation to stem the flows of foreign goods and services, which are generated by underlying competitive conditions, is about as futile as putting a thumb in a very leaky dike. Because this is so, a fair amount of discussion about possible intervention occurs among heads of national banks (those responsible for activating float management) and other key government officials. The purpose of these discussions is to seek agreement about acceptable rates of exchange among currencies (close to competitive equilibrium) and to determine strategies for coordinating float management so that governments are not working at cross-purposes.

International conflict about appropriate exchange rates can arise when several nations pursue fiscal (tax and spending) and monetary policies that are mutually inconsistent. We've already noted that in 1983-84, this type of problem arose because U.S. monetary authorities kept a rather tight lid on monetary growth while the federal budget shifted into a large deficit. This combination is guaranteed to raise interest rates. Financial funds were consequently attracted from abroad by the higher rates paid on deposits in the United States. This flow of funds caused the dollar to become very "strong"—i.e., the dollar's value rose in relation to that of other currencies. "Why complain?" one might ask. Well, as we've seen, when the value of a currency rises, exports become less attractive to foreign customers and their imports become more attractive to us, thereby evoking cries for help from American export industries and sectors that face import competition. We've already examined the seductive attractiveness of trade restrictions and the dangers these pose to the health of world trade, incomes, and employment.

Economists disagreed about whether the 1984 value of the U.S. dollar was out of line with underlying competitive conditions. Those who believed it was out of line called for float intervention (in the form of central bank sales of dollars against other currencies) to reduce the dollar's inflated value. There is, however, general agreement among economists that this sort of problem is inevitable when nations do not actively coordinate their respective fiscal and monetary policies. As we've just seen, high U.S. federal deficits combined with a restrictive monetary policy caused poor export markets for U.S. products (such as agricultural goods) in 1984. They also caused credit markets in Europe to be relatively tight, since funds flowed out of European banks and into U.S. institutions able to pay high interest rates. Europeans then became concerned about the effect that their own tight credit markets would have on the prospects for Europe's full recovery from the long and deep world recession of the early 1980s.

Obviously, the threats of rising waves of protectionism in the United States and of a weak European recovery endangering recovery of the U.S. economy can best be defused by more serious and extensive attempts among the nations involved to coordinate their fiscal, monetary, and exchange-rate policies. Such coordination in 1984, for instance, could have entailed general agreement of the following sort.[8] The United States would reduce its federal deficit and pursue modest monetary expansion, which together would lower U.S. interest rates and thereby remove an important obstacle to full economic recovery here and abroad. European nations would then be able to confidently stimulate their economic recovery by increasing the growth of the domestic monetary supply without fears that financial capital would continue to gravitate toward U.S. markets.

Policy coordination of this sort is much more likely to facilitate full economic recovery of all the world's economies (without a return to high

---

8. Bergsten, "Can We Prevent a World Crisis?" pp. 23ff.

inflation rates) than are independently pursued policies inspired only by narrowly conceived national interests. To work for such collaboration is not a hopeless cause, nor one without precedent. National central bankers already consult with each other, and national political leaders hold economic summits from time to time. In addition, nation members of Europe's Common Market are formally committed to engage in extensive discussion and coordination of monetary, fiscal, and other economic policies. These are encouraging signs, but no one knows when we'll see the day of similar coordination among a larger group of nations.

International trade and finance are extremely complex, and here we've only scratched the surface of them. Significantly, the key theme of this chapter has been the necessity of recognizing economic interdependence among nations. We have seen how isolationist economic policies are at least as unproductive and dangerous as political isolationism. The interdependence that results from relatively free flows of money, goods, and services must be taken into account when national policies affecting these flows are formulated. Institutionalized arrangements for coordinating fiscal, monetary, trade, and exchange-rate policies are probably necessary if international interdependence is to produce the fullest benefits for all nations. Such coordination is based on, and protects, the notion that interdependence can mean "their strength is our good" and vice versa.

IMPLICATIONS

Though we have not defined an explicitly Christian approach to international economic exchange, some conclusions based on a Christian perspective can be drawn. Interdependence is, of course, a crucial biblical theme. The first real economists, born and bred within the English branch of Christendom, liked to point to the "natural harmonies" of marketplace exchanges and trade as examples of divine planning. After all, trade is a form of sharing in which we all benefit by supplying each other with those goods and services that each of us is in the best position to produce. Earlier we noted that even if one party in an exchange has strictly selfish intentions, vigorous market competition forces that party to look out for the best interests of the customers, lest someone else offer them a better deal.

Perhaps Adam Smith's exuberant claim that trade bears the imprint of the divine hand at work in shaping society for the mutual good of all is excessive. Trade is not an unqualified blessing, after all. For instance, it does not by itself insure that the mutual wants served are morally acceptable. Even the benefits of competition do not protect people from trading in heroin or contracting the services of soldiers of fortune. However, despite the limitations of trade, it is perhaps not too much to say that trade is very important as a vehicle for directly caring for others' needs. It also adds to the material abundance that we can use to charitably meet our obligation to love our neighbor—whether across the fence or across the seas. Furthermore, trade enables us to better conserve scarce resources. Finally, free international exchange can break down provincial barriers of thought, culture, and loyalty that otherwise divide the world's peoples. This is what we mean when we suggest that trade is a significant vehicle for materially expressing our interdependence within the human family.

Another lesson we ought to be able to draw from this study of international economic exchanges is that Christians should urge their governments to resist protectionism and to assume leadership in international negotiations leading to freer trade. We should take this stand not only because it serves our best interests as consumers, but also because it recognizes foreigners as neighbors in God's kingdom who should not be taken advantage of for strictly nationalist reasons. Spiritual brotherhood and sisterhood extending across national borders leave no room for protectionist measures based purely on parochial interest and advantage. We believe it is wrong to prevent a skilled minority craftsman from working in a unionized and white-dominated sector. Is it not as wrong to refuse fair market entry to the products of our poorer foreign neighbors?

On the stage of international financial markets in the 1980s (as we saw in Chapter Five), this same moral issue raises its head when some people adopt a callous attitude toward the burdensome debt-repayment problems of Third World countries. These countries are in particular need of understanding and assistance because the prospects of their debt repayment were dealt a triple blow by a long worldwide recession, high U.S. interest rates, and the threat of new protectionist measures against their exports. These nations obviously cannot pay their debts without some combination of relaxed repayment terms and a return to a healthier world economy in which higher export sales can earn them the foreign currency they need to pay the interest and principal on their development loans.

Christians, who understand that in God's kingdom there is no equivalent to national borders that separate peoples, should be glad to know that the moral benefits of free international exchange are complemented by the material benefits of such exchange. Consequently, in their positions as citizens and policymakers, Christians can effectively support on moral grounds the secular arguments for freer economic exchanges among nations and for international coordination of policies affecting these exchanges. International economic exchange and collaboration in shaping it are important means by which we can avoid "beggaring" our foreign neighbors for the sake of advantages afforded to certain home groups. Seen in this light, trade and financial exchanges across borders indeed become material expressions of our human interdependence under God.

Questions for Further Consideration

1. Are you persuaded that exchange produces benefits for both parties involved in it? Is international trade any different in this respect than domestic exchange? If not, why does it raise many more cries of "exploitation"?

2. If trade is good for national economic health, why do nations so easily succumb to protectionist pressures? The fable that opens this chapter, written by a Frenchman in the 1840s, illustrates how ancient and seductive are the appeals for trade protection.

3. What moral and political forces can be effectively marshaled on behalf of freer economic exchange among nations? Who are the modern protagonists of both the fable opening this chapter and the fable of the candlemakers?

4. Why is the public recognition of international interdependence important to both national interests and neighborly concerns?

CHAPTER NINE

Government's Difficult Role in the Economy: Providing for Stability and Growth

From the Conservative point of view, unemployment is logically unnecessary. In an economy left to its own devices, involuntary unemployment can result only from short-run market readjustments.

Robert Carson, *Macro-Economic Issues Today*

But this *long run* is a misleading guide to current affairs. *In the long run* we are all dead. Economists set themselves too easy, too useless a task if in tempestuous seasons they can only tell us that when the storm is long past the ocean is flat again.

John Maynard Keynes, *A Tract on Monetary Reform*

In the United States, Keynesian medicine, demand tonics masquerading as supply-side nostrums, serendipitously administered by anti-Keynesian doctors, revitalized the sick patient.

James Tobin, "The Fiscal Revolution," *Challenge*, Jan.-Feb. 1985

The potency of fiscal policy—both good and bad—has been demonstrated time and again in the past couple of decades.

Walter W. Heller, quoted in *Macro-Economic Issues Today*

Is fiscal policy being oversold? Is monetary policy being oversold? . . . My answer is yes to both of those questions.

Milton Friedman, quoted in *Macro-Economic Issues Today*

Since the Great Depression, national governments have increasingly assumed major responsibility for guiding their economies toward the objective of stable economic growth. Previously, their accepted economic role was limited to raising and allocating the tax revenues needed to provide citizens with those social goods given priority by voters. So, for instance, it has long been recognized that national defense (which thus far in the 1980s has accounted for about 30 percent of U.S. federal spending) and the administration of justice (police, courts, and prisons) cannot be adequately financed through the market sector or by private voluntary donations alone. These activities therefore deserve to be funded by tax payments from all citizens.

The involvement of state and local governments in funding transportation networks, public education and recreational facilities, and fire protection has also long been justified by parallel arguments concerning the likelihood that the perceived need for these services could not be met by private voluntary support and for-profit production alone. Today, federal government expenditures in support of scientific research, space exploration, energy conservation, and environmental protection are largely justified on similar grounds. Furthermore, for generations governments at various levels have also undertaken efforts to assist the poor—efforts ranging from workhouses and parish relief taxes in the late eighteenth century to extensive in-kind and income grants to the poor of our own day.

What is new in the twentieth century is the widespread belief that federal governments have the responsibility and potential ability to manage the overall levels and timing of their expenditures, taxation, and money creation. The generally accepted purposes of such policy management are to promote high employment, prevent high rates of inflation, and provide incentives (or eliminate disincentives) for reasonable economic growth. Prior to the Great Depression, it was assumed that while national governments were responsible for keeping the growth rate of their domestic money supplies consistent with reasonably stable prices, unemployment levels must be left to the vicissitudes of the marketplace.

Recessions and even long depressions periodically plagued Western market economies throughout the nineteenth century. Yet, with few exceptions, classical economists reasoned that such lapses were self-correcting and that their famous rule of "laissez-faire" (by which governments were urged to keep their hands off private domestic and foreign trade) was equally applicable when unemployment levels occasionally reached high levels. A self-correcting mechanism was expected to reverse any general decrease in economic activity. Falling interest rates, prices, and wage rates would eventually permit a return to full-employment output by stimulating investment, consumer purchases, and hiring. In the twentieth century, the supposed natural tendency of an economy to maintain a healthy stability has been called into question.

TWENTIETH-CENTURY GOVERNMENTS ACCEPT RESPONSIBILITY FOR COUNTERING HIGH UNEMPLOYMENT AND INFLATION

With the dramatic advent of *The General Theory of Employment, Interest, and Money,* John Maynard Keynes's 1936 masterpiece on employment and income, economic thinking began to change. While Keynes readily admitted that some self-correcting mechanisms do exist in market economies, he held that they are relatively weak. He believed that it is morally unacceptable to wait for the working out of "natural" correcting mechanisms, which might take a long time to fully eliminate high cyclical unemployment levels.[1] He argued that active economic policies could and should be employed to produce a more rapid recovery. Why wait for a long-run adjustment, he asked, when "in the long run we are all dead"?

The interventionist policy that Keynes recommended for ending the Great Depression was increased spending by federal governments, financed with borrowed—not taxed—funds. This became popularly known as "pump-priming," because increased government spending would put new income into the hands of consumers, who would in turn spend more. Higher sales would do more to stimulate business investment in new plants, equipment, and inventories than would the low, depression-level interest rates available for capital loans to businesses. Increased spending by the government, consumers, and businesses would feed a total growth in incomes several times the size of the initial increase in government spending, thereby returning national economic output to full employment levels.

Keynes's ideas became the principal foundation for post–World War II thinking about how federal governments in market economies should use fiscal and monetary policies to protect their economies against the onset of another deep depression. Most economists contend that the absence of any deep depression since the 1930s is strong evidence of the effectiveness of economic policies originally inspired by the work of Keynes. Since World War II, these policy tools have taken the form of higher government spending and/or lower taxes (e.g., President Kennedy's 1964 tax cut) whenever significant economic slack has occurred, complemented by greater monetary (credit) ease. Thus, the stimulating economic impact of higher government expenditures has been augmented both by the positive effect of lower taxes on consumer spending and by the positive effect of low-interest credit on investment levels. Whenever inflation has resulted from demand growing so rapidly that production could not keep up with it, the reverse of all these policies has been called for—namely, lower government spending, higher taxes, and tighter money and credit.

---

1. Of course, not all unemployment results from inadequate total spending. Neither "frictional unemployment" (which exists because there will always be some workers moving between jobs) nor "structural unemployment" (which results from a mismatch of skills to job requirements as demand for labor shifts away from certain industries and regions and toward others) is much affected by economic expansions and contractions.

This approach became the straightforward, newly "orthodox" prescription for economic stability with high employment and low inflation. Economists disagreed among themselves, varying in the degree to which they preferred monetary/credit policy tools (directed by the Federal Reserve or another central bank) or fiscal policy tools like tax and spending changes. Their differences hinged on varied estimates of how rapidly the desired policy changes could be made and how effective they would be in eliminating the causes of a particular economic malady (inflation or unemployment). For instance, they had varying responses to the fact that, while monetary/credit policy has an advantage over tax and spending policy in terms of implementation speed, it is at times a weak instrument to stimulate demand. (In a depression, businesses can be brought to a plentiful credit trough, but they can't be made to borrow and spend for expansion.)

Differences among economists also grew out of conflicting values regarding what share of total economic activity belonged in the public sector. Increased government spending does provide a potentially more powerful stimulus to a sagging economy than either increased credit or lower taxes, but it simultaneously enlarges the public sector relative to the private sector. On the other hand, various mixes of both fiscal and monetary restraint are sometimes recommended by economists for reasons unrelated to their personal preferences about the proper size of government. These reasons include worries about how interest rates will be affected by too much spending plus too much monetary restraint, since interest rates affect foreign credit flows and import competition as well as the health of certain domestic industries like housing. This was proven as recently as 1984, when large fiscal deficits, combined with anti-inflationary monetary restraint, produced high interest rates. These rates hurt both interest-sensitive domestic industries and exports.

A NEW PROBLEM RAISES QUESTIONS ABOUT THE FEDERAL GOVERNMENT'S ROLE IN STABILIZATION

In the late 1970s and early 1980s, the troublesome double crises of high inflation and high unemployment in most industrial market economies led some economists to claim that Keynesian economic analysis and policy prescriptions were dead, or at least dying. The apparent puzzle was how inflation (previously associated with *excess* demand) and unemployment (previously associated with *insufficient* demand) could exist simultaneously. Furthermore, a policy prescription for unemployment—namely, fiscal and monetary stimulation—was obviously *not* what the economic doctors had ever ordered for combating inflation.

A new doctrine emerged, one that vied seriously for political ascendancy but contended less seriously for academic respectability. It became known as supply-side economics. Advocates claimed that Keynesian-inspired policies—which had focused on manipulating overall demand by altering taxes, government spending levels, and the money supply—were seriously misguided. "Supply-siders" were convinced that active manipulation of government spending levels and taxes for stabilization purposes was responsible for an unhealthy growth in government's share in the U.S. economy since the Depression. (In reality, the use of Keynesian stabilization tools does not require "big government," nor does it necessarily cause big government.) The key supply-side theme was that supply, not demand, was crucial to economic health, and that liberal Keynesian fiscal and monetary policies had actually weakened the otherwise healthy sources of supply. Supply-siders believed that high taxes had dampened incentives to work and produce, that heavy government borrowing had squeezed out borrowing by private businesses for innovation and expansion, and that high rates of inflation had penalized thrifty people, whose hard-earned savings were worth less every year.

The supply-side prescription for dealing with *both* unemployment and inflation was a single package of policies, all designed to stimulate the growth of output (supply). The prescription called for decreased government spending and lower tax rates, which would leave more room for private-sector production and consumption. Proponents expected that lower tax rates would restore some incentives for people to work and to take risks in order to earn higher wages and profits. They also expected lower welfare payments to restore the incentive (or the necessity) for the poor to work hard and spend responsibly. In addition, they generally favored expansionary monetary policy in hopes that faster rates of monetary growth would reduce interest rates, thereby stimulating investment and growth of output. They believed that such output growth would reduce inflation, which in turn would promote the higher levels of personal saving needed to fund long-term business investment.

There is actually nothing novel about most supply-side proposals. They represent classical (nineteenth-century) economic thinking about the key role that incentives to work, save, invest, and produce play in the promotion of long-term, healthy economic growth. What *does* distinguish supply-side from Keynesian-inspired thinking and policies is supply-siders' apparent belief that the best prescriptions for long-term growth will also work wonders in dealing with short-term cyclical problems like high unemployment and inflation. Supply-side policies are supposed to reduce unemployment and inflation by stimulating economic expansion. But available evidence concerning their impact on work effort, saving, and so forth suggests that these policies take effect only slowly and that their effect is ultimately small. (For instance, a substantial 25 percent cut in marginal tax rates for a typical household would result in family wage earners together adding only 2 percent to their hours worked—about forty-five minutes per week.)[2] Thus, supply-side policies have greater potential for enhancing long-term growth prospects than for combating short-term problems of cyclical unemployment or high inflation. Consequently, most economists believe that the tools of fiscal and monetary policy should still be employed to accomplish short-run stabilization. Demand should be siphoned off (with higher taxes and/or lower government spending, and monetary/credit restraint) when it appears to be building so rapidly that inflation will be sparked. When the economy is suffering from high unemployment and low capacity utilization, the opposite steps should be taken to stimulate demand.

Some critics of so-called "countercyclical" fiscal and monetary policy for economic stabilization (the approach inspired by Keynes) argue that the very manipulations of taxes, spending, and money/credit supply have themselves been a primary cause of economic instability in the past two decades. They claim that countercyclical policies, though well-intentioned, have made the business environment *less* predictable, and that such policies have been biased in favor of inflationary stimulation of the economy through more government spending and increased money-supply growth. At times these critics appear to blame the simultaneous high inflation and high unemployment experienced in the 1970s and early 1980s on misguided Keynesian manipulation of fiscal and monetary tools for stabilization purposes.

Most economists agree that rapid "stop-go" policy approaches to stabilization—such that one minute the fiscal/monetary acceleration pedal is being pushed to the floor, and the next minute the fiscal/monetary brakes are being applied—are bad. In the 1970s they probably hurt economic growth and thereby prevented a return to the relatively modest inflation rates and low unemployment levels of the past. However, most economists believe that the acute combination of high, rising inflation and disturbingly resistant high unemployment levels in the 1970s cannot be attributed solely to mismanagement of countercyclical fiscal and monetary tools.

The inflationary pressures that built up in the late 1960s and early 1970s

2. See Edgar K. Browning and Jacquelene M. Browning, *Public Finance and the Price System* (New York: Macmillan, 1983), p. 443.

resulted initially from the all-too-common problem of America's wanting to spend on war without paying for it in higher taxes. (It's not so much Keynesian policy as war that has a built-in inflationary bias.) To this explanation of inflation—on the basis of excessive demand induced by deficit spending—must be added the experience in the 1970s with inflationary shocks on the supply side. Rising oil prices, coupled with some shortfalls in food production, worked their way through the economy, forcing up the cost of products dependent on oil and raising the cost of living for consumers. Workers then sought to protect themselves from inflation by vigorously bargaining for wage increases to cover anticipated price increases or by asking for automatic cost-of-living adjustments in their salaries.

Expectations of inflation on the part of workers and producers were written into labor contracts and affected pricing decisions. Taken together, the measures people used to protect themselves from anticipated inflation made effective stabilization policies much more difficult. If it wanted to keep unemployment at acceptable low levels, the federal government had to use fiscal and monetary policies to sustain already overheated demand. If, on the other hand, it chose to fight inflation, built-in inflationary expectations made the task much more costly in terms of recession and high unemployment needed to cool off the economy.

Furthermore, because the causes of inflation came from both the supply side (shortages) and demand side (rising military and social expenditures), the ordinary Keynesian prescription for dealing with inflation—namely, higher taxes, reduced government spending, and tighter credit—posed an acute dilemma. Restrictive fiscal and monetary policies would create much more unemployment than they did when they were used to fight inflation resulting from excess demand alone. And even when policymakers "bit the bullet," the unusually high levels of unemployment caused by restrictive policies soon generated overwhelming cries for a reversal of these policies in order to deal with rising unemployment (which replaced inflation as "Public Enemy Number One"). This is the story of what happened over the 1970s—policy vacillated between the extremes of stimulation and contraction as popular displeasure shifted back and forth from unemployment to inflation.

A VERDICT IN FAVOR OF CONTINUED
GOVERNMENT USE OF STABILIZATION TOOLS
COUPLED WITH REVITALIZED INCENTIVES

What does all this mean? Should countercyclical fiscal and monetary policies be abandoned as worthless, even harmful? There is honest disagreement about the matter. Nobel prizewinning economist Milton

Friedman and other conservative economists (including many supply-siders) argue that fiscal and monetary tools ought to be used to shape long-run economic trends, and that cyclical deviations from these trends should not be tinkered with. They believe that the discretionary use of fiscal and monetary tools is often mistimed due to lags in accurately perceiving the economic problem at hand, delays in making the needed policy change, and the slow rate at which the economy responds to the policy change. Their solution: If the government maintains a hands-off position, the economy will cure itself of inflationary and recessionary ills as people adjust their expectations and prices to new realities.

Friedman recommends that the Federal Reserve Bank simply agree to permit money supply growth at a constant rate consistent with long-run economic growth (e.g., 3 percent annually). He suggests that monetary authorities forswear any attempt to stimulate the economy when a recession occurs or to rein in the economy when inflation proves to be a problem. With respect to fiscal policy, Friedman recommends that both taxes and spending be reduced so that total government involvement in the economy diminishes and makes room for the private sector to bloom.

A majority of economists probably disagree with the prescription of pure steady-as-you-go fiscal and monetary policies and the consequent abandonment of any attempt to use these tools as an economic ballast against high inflation and high unemployment. These economists recognize that fiscal and monetary policy seemed unable to deal with the twin devils of inflation and unemployment in the 1970s, but they ascribe this apparent impotence to rising social demands and the increasingly inflexible responses of wages and prices to changing economic conditions. So, for instance, rising social demands made Americans willing to conduct a war without either raising taxes or reducing social expenditures sufficiently to finance it. And, of course, once inflation became a big enough nuisance to warrant concern, workers and others sought to protect themselves against inflationary "theft" of their purchasing power by demanding that built-in price escalators be provided for wages, social security, and so forth. In the presence of an economic downturn, however, upward momentum built into wages meant that *employment,* not wages, suffered most from reduced demand. Furthermore, other price-and-wage rigidities in uncompetitive, regulated industries also directly reduced the ability of macro-economic policies to fight inflation. And the lack of competition in these industries actually aggravated inflation by reducing productivity gains in these sectors.

Thus it is often argued that fiscal and monetary stabilization policies need not be abandoned if excessive (unfundable) demands on the public purse are eliminated and if steps are taken to increase price and wage flexibility and to improve overall productivity growth in the economy. Some of the popularity of proposed laws (or Constitutional amendments) requiring an automatic balanced budget stems from a desire to forcibly keep public spending within the bounds of realizable tax revenues. Some of these proposals would prevent the use of tax and spending changes to stabilize an economy suffering from either recession or overheated expansion. (The Gramm-Rudman bill, passed in 1985, is a type of balanced budget law, but its purpose is emergency deficit control.) However, fiscal responsibility (living within the public means) need not rule out using taxes and spending to increase economic stability. Deficits necessary to stimulate recovery in a very weak economy could later be matched by surpluses during periods of economic expansion, when a federal budget surplus is needed to prevent overheating.

A law restraining budget deficits can force the federal government to show "fiscal discipline," but what is most needed for fiscal responsibility is open public debate about spending and tax priorities. Voters must realize, and legislators must acknowledge, the irresponsibility of expecting governments to undertake more tasks (or the same tasks at higher levels) without either providing the necessary additional funds or cutting back on expenditures for some existing programs. The problems with inflation and unemployment in the 1970s were a product of excessive demands upon the public purse (and upon regulatory powers) to support a war, provide income maintenance, furnish health and environmental protection, and so forth. Consequently, public debate over acceptable priorities for allocating pieces of the finite fiscal pie are crucial to solving those problems. Ultimately, fostering this ongoing debate is more important and honest than passing a strictly binding law requiring a balanced budget.

In the realm of increased price and wage flexibility, many economists, conservative and liberal alike, agree that taking steps to increase competitiveness in various markets is important, because competition stimulates productivity and lowers prices. The deregulatory wave in transport, communications, and banking that was begun during President Carter's term is an example of economists from different camps pinning greater hopes on free markets. Some economists also advocate the use of certain tax incentives that would induce workers to hold down wage demands and induce producers to hold down price increases during an inflationary period. The hope is that such incentives would persuade workers, producers, and consumers to "bet on" an end to inflation and thereby behave in ways that would actually reduce inflationary pressures. And all economists agree that opposing protectionism in foreign trade is crucial to winning any inflationary battle. Reduced trade barriers can stimulate economic adjustment to changing market conditions and promote a return to economic growth in this and other countries.

SUPPLY-SIDE CLAIMS AND THE 1980S DEFICIT

Just as some excessive hopes for Keynesian-style approaches to economic stabilization grew up in the post–World War II period (undampened by any realistic sense of the impact of cumulative demands upon the government's purse), so also excessive hopes have been pinned on supply-side proposals in recent years. President Reagan entered office on an explicitly supply-side platform, calling for both reduced spending and reduced taxes. He also embraced a supply-side strategy, calling first for reduced taxes. He hoped that Congress would thereafter feel forced to adopt spending cuts consistent with the lower tax revenues. Reagan's proposed tax cuts were adopted, but what ensued on the expenditure side did not follow the supply-side prescription, despite the administration's proclaimed belief in supply-side cures.

The administration shifted budget priorities from social programs to defense but did not reduce overall expenditures. (Federal expenditures as a share of the GNP actually rose slightly during Reagan's first term.) Consequently, tax decreases, unmatched by expenditure reductions, greatly increased the budget deficit. Ironically, this is the very approach (though on a much greater scale) suggested by Keynesian, *not* supply-side, policy in order to counteract a recession like that of 1981-82. Unfortunately, stimulation was lopsided, since a large and growing deficit was accompanied by stingy monetary/credit growth. The two combined to produce a situation in which government's borrowing to finance the federal deficit elbowed out some private-sector borrowing from the same financial pool. This was reflected in very high interest rates. As always, high interest rates hit certain sectors of the economy very hard—especially housing, where demand is particularly sensitive to interest rates. Export industries also suffered, because their ability to compete in world markets was severely hurt when high interest rates contributed to the dollar's rise relative to other currencies.

The public's confusion about what fiscal and monetary policies made sense for the mid-1980s was aggravated by the bizarre presidential campaign of 1984. The Democratic candidate found himself advocating greater fiscal responsibility by proposing a partial reversal of earlier tax cuts. Historically this was an unusual proposal for a Democrat to make, but it was also a perfectly orthodox Keynesian remedy for excessive buildup of demand. As the Republican candidate, however, Reagan stood behind his own tax and spending program, which looked much more like an overdone Keynesian solution to recession than a supply-side solution to all economic ills.

To compound the confusion, the Democratic candidate talked of the need to protect the U.S. automobile industry with "domestic content" and other legislative action, a characteristically Democratic posture arising out of the belief that such measures protect labor. Reagan, on the other hand, claiming to be relatively free of political debts to organized labor and an ardent defender of free markets, remained silent about the protectionist trade measures his own administration had enacted during his first four years in office. Given this scenario, the public could perhaps be forgiven if it was confused about where truth, justice, and accurate economic predictions lay. An ideologically supply-side administration was practicing haphazard Keynesian remedies without acknowledging it, and the Democratic challenger appeared to embrace a fiscal conservatism for which his party had never been known.

It was obvious that once the political dust settled after the 1984 campaign, the anomaly of high deficits and restrictive monetary policy would have to be vigorously addressed. This is not essentially a partisan issue. Certain steps must be taken to reduce the deficit. President Reagan is urging nondefense budget cuts as the best path. However, simple feasibility considerations suggest that the task is too great to be accomplished with either budget cuts or tax increases alone. The Brookings Institution has produced an excellent survey of possibilities for across-the-board reductions in the rate of growth of public spending, longer-term restructuring of expenditures, short-term tax surcharges, and longer-term tax reform. According to the survey, sole reliance on tax changes would require an annual tax increase of five thousand dollars per family in order to eliminate the budget deficit by the end of the 1980s; sole reliance on budget cuts to eliminate the deficit would require a 25 percent reduction in total federal expenditures.[3] Clearly, either of these approaches would be intolerable. If, on the other hand, the necessary sacrifices were spread across spending categories and allocated among tax-paying groups, the same goal could be accomplished with much less drastic dislocation.

The Brookings study was done by a group of very highly regarded economists who do not argue on behalf of any political party or any narrow economic ideology. Realism requires that the immediate burdens of expenditure freezes or cuts must be widely shared if they are going to

3. See *Economic Choices 1984*, ed. Alice M. Rivlin (Washington: The Brookings Institution, 1984), p. 38.

pass political muster. Recent experience with Social Security and Medicare programs, federal retirement benefits, and agricultural subsidies suggests that important changes in these programs can be made in order to reduce their budgetary burden (or their rate of growth vis-à-vis other categories). If high interest rates are to be kept from adding tremendously to deficit financing costs, then it will be important to take immediate steps that will temporarily freeze expenditure growth and introduce a general tax surcharge. In the longer run it will be necessary to restructure taxes as well as expenditures. The twofold purpose of tax changes should be (1) to help eliminate the deficit from the revenue side and (2) to restructure the vast array of inequitable and highly distortional taxes.

PROPOSED TAX REFORMS—THEIR POTENTIAL CONTRIBUTIONS TO DEFICIT REDUCTION, FAIRNESS, AND GROWTH

It is particularly in the realm of tax reform that Americans have an opportunity and a responsibility to see that high social values are reflected in eventual changes of the federal tax system. Since Adam Smith wrote on the subject in 1776, widely acknowledged principles of taxation have included both "fairness" in distributing the tax burden and "efficiency" in raising revenues. The existing federal tax system departs unduly from both these criteria. The complex array of existing tax loopholes (consisting of exclusions and deductions) frequently results in persons with the same incomes being taxed differently, and it also gives the most favorable treatment to people with higher incomes. This tax structure is an obvious violation of the fairness principle, since it results in an inequitable sharing of the tax burden. It also produces disturbing inefficiencies, since financial and other resources are artificially drawn into the sheltered sectors, thereby reducing economic growth.

It is generally agreed, for example, that tax loopholes (such as investment tax credits) and other variations in tax rates by type of investment distort investment decisions in favor of less productive sectors. This can easily reduce the potential return on total new investment by 80 percent! Consider Figure 1, in which three types of investment are compared. Investment type A must pay an 80 percent tax on returns, B a 40 percent tax, and C zero tax. The shaded areas represent taxes paid out of market returns. In order for all these types of investment to effectively compete with each other for funds, they must offer the same after-tax returns (unshaded portions). But if the rate of return on investment type A falls by only 1 percent, it will lose funds to investment types B and C. Thus tax

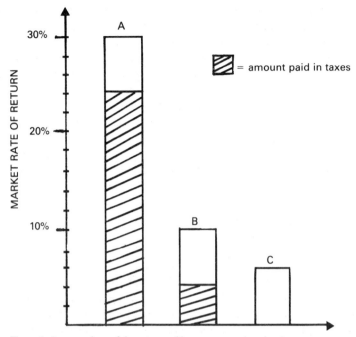

Figure 1. A comparison of three types of investments and tax burdens

discrimination makes investment type A a "loser," even though when measured by its rate of return, this type of investment is still much more productive for society than investment type C.[4]

Some loopholes also distort worker compensation packages by encouraging a shift toward more nonwage benefits. Other loopholes favor saving in certain instruments (like retirement accounts) at the expense of others. The tax laws not only distort savings but also reduce their level, since income taxes on interest earnings may discourage people from saving to provide for their own future support. For instance, in the absence of an income tax, a person setting aside income for retirement thirty-five years hence would sacrifice thirty-five dollars of current income to provide himself or herself with one thousand dollars of future income (assuming a 10 percent annual rate of return on savings). However, with a 30 percent income tax, this person would have to sacrifice three times as much current income to achieve the same objec-

4. See *Economic Choices 1984,* p. 104.

tive in retirement income. Obviously, such an income-tax bite may lead some people to save less toward retirement.

By restricting the tax base, the plethora of loopholes necessitates a heavier tax burden on wages, which in turn penalizes work. Furthermore, the complex array of loopholes sometimes makes expenditures aimed at finding ways to skirt taxes more profitable than expenditures on innovation, cost cutting, and better marketing![5]

There are a number of tax reform proposals contending for congressional and public attention. Recently, discussion of some form of a "flat tax" on incomes has achieved some popularity. A flat tax is designed to eliminate income-tax brackets (and the higher the bracket, the higher the tax rate) and abolish existing deductions and exemptions. This means that everyone—both the rich and those with modest incomes—would pay out the same percent of their incomes in taxes. By eliminating deductions and exclusions, the flat tax would broaden the tax base and eliminate many of the inefficient distortions caused by the existing tax system. However, the flat tax would be a dramatic departure from the long-held public belief that a "fair" sharing of the tax burden is one in which the wealthy contribute a greater proportion of their resources to support the government than do those who are less well-off. Any such departure demands that careful consideration be given to the implied shift in public values. (For this very reason, current proposals for a flat tax are not advocating a tax that is truly "flat," since they exempt people with very low incomes and maintain a limited number of tax brackets.)

A number of economists are proposing that taxes on income and corporate profits be replaced with expenditure and cash-flow taxes (with built-in progressive tax brackets). Such a comprehensive tax reform would mean that individuals would pay taxes on their expenditures (income minus savings) and corporations would pay taxes on their incomes (revenues minus all expenses, including those on investment). This shift, combined with the elimination of all or most existing deductions and exemptions, would result in a great broadening of the tax base (thereby enabling equal or greater revenues to be generated with lower tax *rates*) and would also rectify the inefficient distortions mentioned earlier. If enacted, therefore, the reform could be expected to promote economic growth by restoring incentives for work, saving, and highly productive investment. At the same time, the reform would remove much of the unfairness built into the existing tax system. Like any plan for comprehensive reform, the expenditure/cash-flow proposal will generate op-

5. For a good discussion of these points, see chap. 5 of *Economic Choices 1984*.

position from those who benefit most under existing tax exemptions and deductions. However, this approach to tax reform deserves close public attention, since it would increase tax simplicity, efficiency, and fairness while also providing needed increases in revenues.

A short recap of this chapter's discussion thus far reveals the necessity of revamping current spending and tax structures. We've noted that recent economic history still points to a need for federal governments to use fiscal and monetary policy tools in the interest of economic stability (which means low unemployment and low inflation)—an opinion shared by most economists. We've also indicated that establishing such equilibrium is far from easy. Witness the high and rising federal deficits in the mid-1980s, wreaking havoc with important sectors of the American economy. A way out of the morass by the end of the 1980s will require both short-term and long-term restructuring of federal expenditures and reform of the federal tax system. We've seen that a good tax reform is one that in the interest of greater efficiency lowers and standardizes tax rates across similar categories and, in the interest of fairness, imposes a lesser burden on the incomes of the poor than it does on the incomes of the rich. Happily, taken together, these recommended changes in federal spending and taxation offer some promise of removing certain barriers to economic growth (in the form of low savings, distorted investment, etc.), which itself is crucial to economic stability.

GOVERNMENTS' RESPONSIBILITY TO PROMOTE GROWTH—A MISPLACED OR UNACHIEVABLE GOAL?

One question remains: "What role should governments play in fostering economic growth?" Of all the roles of government discussed so far in this chapter, government's potential role with respect to economic growth is the least understood by Christians who are otherwise very sensitive to the issues of poverty and justice surrounding unemployment and inflation and the instruments used for their alleviation—namely, taxation and government spending. Why has the pursuit of economic growth received such a negative response from these people? Several factors are involved. Critics of growth are pessimistic about continued availability of the natural resources necessary to growth, and they are concerned about further serious deterioration of the environment. The apparent environmental and resource limits to sustainable long-term growth are interpreted by some Christians as signs of the "dues" our society will pay for the sin of rampant materialism. They usually ignore any contradiction between their dislike of growth and their outspoken support for the goals of low unemployment and more equitable incomes for the poor people of America and the poor nations of the world.

Is this dislike and distrust of a growth goal warranted? Obviously, our answer depends on whether the critics of growth are right when they say that perpetual economic growth is not possible, that it destroys the environment, that it betrays a warped value system, and that it is not necessary to the achievement of other important goals. Economists as a group are predominantly optimistic about the possibilities for continued economic growth into the distant future. Some Christian critics suspect, however, that such optimism is based on a faith in human technical solutions to problems best left in the hands of God. They also believe that economists are the professional group most likely to be sucked into defending a materialistic set of values and motivations. After all, aren't these the people who assume that producers are motivated by profits, who take the GNP to be a crucial measure of a population's well-being, and who build into their theoretical models the notion that "time is money"? From this perspective, economists are the people most likely to "worship" economic growth for its own sake and for the mastery over the universe that it presumes to offer humankind.

Actually, economists are not more materialistic than others in our society. Furthermore, economists are often among the first to deny that the GNP measures everything that is important for the "good life." Tibor Scitovsky, a well-known senior economist, has pointed out that only a small share of what brings happiness actually passes through the marketplace.[6] Professional economists understand (sometimes better than the layperson) that people with a deep capacity for love, laughter, understanding, and selfless service are more apt to enjoy lasting "riches" than people bent on profit and growth at all cost. At the same time, economists believe that economic concerns must be dealt with in order to clear the way for more vital concerns like peace. Most economists are led to believe in the possibility and desirability of continued economic growth not by misplaced pride in human progress and materialism but by history itself.

Economists typically maintain that history does not support the idea that limited natural resources impede growth. In fact, history records many successful transitions from dependence on certain increasingly scarce resources to reliance on other less scarce nonrenewable resources or on better-managed renewable resources. Historical shifts among vari-

6. Scitovsky, *The Joyless Economy: An Inquiry into Human Satisfaction and Consumer Dissatisfaction* (New York: Oxford University Press, 1976), p. 103.

ous energy sources—wood, dung, whale oil, petroleum, coal, and hydro-electric power—are examples of this phenomenon. So also are the developments in long-distance communication, which once relied on a messenger on foot or on horseback or a message transmitted by wire, but now relies on glass fibers, computers, and satellites.

While it is not certain that humankind will be able to develop technical capabilities in response to increased future scarcities, economists know of no compelling reason to believe such development is unlikely to occur. Structural changes that usually accompany growth in a country which is already enjoying a high standard of living also bode well for continued growth, since economic services are performed with less resource-intensive equipment (like transistors) and typically grow as a share of total output. Furthermore, the side effects of increased production polluting air and water resources can and are being controlled in several important instances by various user charges, which induce cleaner production without calling a halt to growth. Where the scarce resource of land is concerned, there are prospects for market-guided (or augmented) land-use decisions that would ensure its availability into the distant future.

It is too early to tell whether economists who are optimistic about the prospects of future growth will have the last word. They are undoubtedly right, however, in believing that economic growth will not suddenly come to a halt with some catastrophic using up of most key resources. Long before a resource like coal is actually used up, its price will rise, thereby providing an incentive for users to conserve on their rates of consumption, for producers to search out substitutes, and for extractive industries to improve techniques for discovering and removing previously unknown (or inaccessible) deposits. If the prices of most natural resources were to begin a steady upward climb, *then* we might indeed want to contemplate whether continued material economic growth was possible. But this has not yet happened. Consequently, we're left with this question: Why do economists think it is so important to promote economic growth and remove unnecessary barriers to growth?

THE IMPORTANT VIRTUES OF GROWTH

We've touched on the answer to this question several times in this chapter and in earlier chapters as well. Poverty is chiefly a matter of an individual's or a nation's having no productive place in the domestic or world economy. People and nations are materially poor because they are not producing and exchanging valuable surpluses with others. Consequently, virtually the only way that the poor can find their way out of poverty, without simply displacing others, is to find a niche for their skills and other resources in an expanding domestic and world economy. For at least the rest of this century, labor forces will continue to grow—because birth rates still exceed death rates, because foreign workers are attracted to the United States by higher earnings, and because women, minorities, and others leave homemaking or subsistence-level activities to seek wage employment and the opportunity of a higher standard of living. But these entrants into the market will not find jobs—they will not create the pieces of the economic pie they hope to eat—unless economic growth continues. The pie must be increasing if they are to find a place at the workbench; once they do so, they can then help create an even bigger pie for the table.

Continued economic growth is important for at least two more related reasons. First, the public's difficult choices between private and public spending are made easier if the cost of more public spending is a slower *rate* of growth in private consumption rather than an absolute decline in dollars spent. (This principle is obvious to anyone who has worked for an organization in which slower budget increases in one area than in another create much less backlash than does a shift of dollars from one category to another within a fixed budget.) This explains why it's much easier to find support for such things as increased expenditures on environmental cleanup, assistance to the poor, and lower trade barriers in a growing economy than in a stagnant one. Second, market economies are continually responding to shifts in demand that are induced by fluctuating tastes, changing income levels, and so forth, and to shifts in supply, such as those that arise with new technologies. Consequently, financial and labor resources are being drawn out of one activity and into another. Without economic growth, which increases the total number of jobs available to individuals and communities, the problems of dislocation and long-term unemployment increase.

Taken together, these reasons suggest that economic growth is an important means whereby new people and new social wants can be accommodated and through which greater job security is also provided to those already at work in an economy. This same reasoning underscores with equal force the desirability of promoting both domestic and worldwide economic growth.

By these lights, national governments should do more than stabilize their economies. They should undertake measures to stimulate growth, for instance, by subsidizing basic research. They should change tax structures (as previously discussed) so that taxes don't unduly crimp saving or draw investment away from the most productive sectors. Even their dedication to stabilization is important to economic growth, since high inflation (and high unemployment) reduces the levels and productivity of investment. The link between stabilization and growth comes full circle with the realization that higher rates of unemployment cannot be prevented (a goal of stabilization policy) unless the pace at which new jobs are created equals the pace at which the prospective labor force grows. Growth and stabilization are mutually supportive goals for economic policy.

A NO TO "GROWTHSMANSHIP"

So far, we've tried to counter some common prejudices against economic growth—that it can't continue and that it's necessarily harmful to our world and our souls. Our conclusion is that government has some responsibility to remove unnecessary barriers to growth and should perhaps spend in some ways that specifically promote growth. Of course, economic growth is not *all* good, nor is the highest feasible rate of growth the one we should necessarily desire and expect governments to promote. Rapid growth (considerably faster than the average per-capita growth of the GNP in this century) cannot occur unless present generations commit themselves to much larger sacrifices than they are making now. They would have to reduce current consumption in order to augment savings and thereby finance the technological innovation and capital expansion that raise productivity, increasing output and per-capita incomes for the future.

People in most societies do save. In the interest of growth they can perhaps be induced to save *more*—for instance, by altering the tax treatment of interest earnings. But for good reasons most societies do not try to *dramatically* improve their overall rate of saving by using taxation, inflation, or pricing interventions to forcibly keep consumption down. Because these measures usually violate common notions of liberty and justice, they are not tolerated in most democracies. After all, the people of this generation are likely to wonder why they should be forced to make heavy sacrifices for the sake of future generations who will probably be much richer than they!

Thus there is a voluntarily determined rate of saving that sets certain limits on how much growth the marketplace can generate. It can be logically argued that governments should try to mildly augment that "natural growth rate." For example, they might subsidize basic research with tax monies on the grounds that private markets are less well-suited to this task than they are to financing technological applications of new ideas. On the other hand, private markets may already promote too much growth, since production decisions ignore certain negative spillover effects for which we don't yet have solutions.

Up until now, the benefits of moderate growth outlined earlier have probably outweighed the eventual environmental costs—and will probably continue to do so into the foreseeable future. But these real costs of growth should be taken as a warning against governments' engaging in vigorous "growthsmanship" policies aimed at forcibly diverting many more resources to growth than does the market (savers and investors) of its own accord. On the other hand, because there are important net advantages to *some* growth, governments certainly should remove any unnecessary barriers to growth, such as those arising from taxing systems that bias saving and investment decisions in favor of ventures with lower rates of return.

CHRISTIAN VALUES IN RELATION TO GOVERNMENTAL GOALS OF ECONOMIC STABILITY WITH GROWTH

What does government's role in guiding the economy have to do with stewardship and other Christian values? We've reasoned that fiscal and monetary policy tools can be usefully applied to the economy in ways that permit greater economic stability. We've used the analogy of ballast, because well-conceived federal taxation, spending, and money supply growth can prevent the economic ship from being wrecked by either inflation's gales or depression's hurricanes. To use another analogy, fiscal and monetary policies act as thermostats. Higher taxes and tighter controls on money supply growth can prevent the overheating of the economy by siphoning off excessive spending. If, instead, the economy is chilled by too little demand and is experiencing high unemployment levels, these policies can be reversed to reinvigorate the economy.

Christians, who generally support the use of modern medical technology and sensible steps toward maintaining good health, should easily understand the rationale for the judicious use of stabilization policies to protect the economic health of a nation. True, bodily health does not stand above all other emotional and spiritual health. But it can fairly be said that bodily health usually complements the fullest expression of other human values. Bodies that are well taken care of usually have the stamina and mental vigor necessary to glorify God in worship and service. The economic health of a society is important in the same way. The economic goals of a stabilization policy—low unemployment and low inflation—are basic to the health of a nation. And when it is in good economic shape, it has the capacity not only to meet the needs of its own people but also to serve the people of other countries.

The Scriptures teach the value and nobility of work (patterned after the formative work of God the Creator), the importance of stewardly management of financial and natural resources, and the virtue of generously sharing our blessings of time, energy, and material goods. It stands to reason, therefore, that Christians should approve of policies aimed at insuring an economy's ability to provide jobs and policies that protect the purchasing power of its citizens. The Great Depression and recent deep recessions have repeatedly reminded us of how crucial work is—not only to meeting basic physical needs but to maintaining one's sense of personhood. Similarly, inflation rates in the 1970s reminded us that rapid price increases make judicious shopping difficult, discourage provident saving against future needs, encourage profligate consumption of resources, and generally shift our attention away from the near or distant future as we scr p over access to goods and pleasures of the present.

There is no single, peculiarly Christian way of defining what government's role ought to be in an economy. There is no economic ideology or sys em which is singularly Christian. Nor is there any uniquely Christian way of doing economic analysis. Throughout this book we have used standard economic reasoning to examine scarcity and to isolate the private and social choices we are faced with as faithful stewards of scarce amounts of time, money, and natural resources. In all times, much economic thought has been devoted to matters of efficiency (getting the most out of what is available) and growth (increasing the size of the economic pie). We can now see that both efficiency and growth are important if we are to responsibly use precious gifts, meet the demands of justice, and imitate the selfless love of God, the creative Giver.

Questions for Further Consideration

1. The quotations that open this chapter represent a variety of approaches to government involvement in economic stabilization. They range from a hands-off policy to activist intervention. As we've seen in this chapter, the policy debate continues. Why has the once unbounded enthusiasm for government intervention waned? Why do most economists nevertheless regard stabilization as a necessary and achievable good for macro-economic policy? Do you agree?

2. Why is the mix of high government expenditures and slow monetary growth that we have seen in the early 1980s such a dangerous one?

3. What possibilities do you favor for reducing the deficit? What role should tax reform play in our economy?

4. Do the virtues of economic growth outweigh the expected costs? What moral grounds, if any, do you find for promoting economic stability along with moderate growth?

5. Is economic efficiency a concern primarily to materialists?

CHAPTER TEN

U.S. Security: Counting the Cost of Military Spending*

Every gun that is made,
every warship launched,
every rocket fired signifies,
in the final sense,
a theft from those who hunger and are not fed;
those who are cold, and are not clothed.

Dwight D. Eisenhower

it will be a great day
when
our schools
get all the money
they need
and the air force
has to hold
a bake sale
to buy a
bomber.

Anonymous

National defense must be our highest priority. Our military strength preserves and defends our freedom and sustains the peace. Cutting the defense budget at a time of further Soviet modernization and expansion of its military budget imperils our national security and sells the American people short.

Republican National Committee

People feel insecure for many reasons—economic as well as military. In the late 1970s, the most widely discussed insecurities concerned jacked-up oil prices and escalating inflation. By the early 1980s, rising unemployment became a primary source of insecurity for many families in the United States and other nations affected by two worldwide recessions. Adding to these sources of insecurity has been a widespread grassroots concern over risks of nuclear warfare.

Insecurity is a very distressing feeling against which individuals and nations try to protect themselves. Families buy insurance to protect them-

*This chapter was significantly influenced and shaped by Dan Ebels, former professor of economics at Hope College.

selves against some types of financial insecurity. Grain farmers deal in the futures market to protect themselves against adverse price changes for a portion of their crops. And national governments, as we discussed in Chapter Nine, typically use fiscal and monetary measures to reduce the incidence of high inflation or high unemployment, thereby improving the economic security of millions of households. In addition to attempting to prevent widespread unemployment, modern governments also use various benefit programs to reduce the financial insecurities of families who already face temporary unemployment or poverty.

The topic of this chapter is military spending, another type of expenditure that governments make to increase the security of their citizens. This is a subject that excites vigorous debate among political leaders, certain interest groups, and members of the press. Unfortunately, the average citizen finds it difficult to separate facts from passions when national defense and military spending are being discussed. How real, we wonder, are these threats against which we are expected to spend and pay with our taxes? And are we getting the level of security we want with the dollars the military spends?

Christians aren't spared the agony of deciding where truth lies in these debates. We are pulled between two extremes. Christian pacifists ask us to refuse to pay that large portion—about one-third—of our tax dollar that supports the military. They argue that building up arms, even for defense, is directly contrary to the teachings of Jesus, the Prince of Peace. At the other extreme are Christians who are convinced that Russia is the "evil empire" against which Christian America must vigorously prepare to defend itself and the rest of the free world.

Somewhere in the middle are the confused majority of Christians. Like the prophet Isaiah, they know their ultimate security is not in arms and alliances: "Woe to those who go down to Egypt for help and rely on horses, who trust in chariots because they are many and in horsemen because they are very strong, but do not look to the Holy One of Israel or consult the Lord!" (Isa. 31:1). Yet these same Christians of the middle ground believe that biblical counsels of prudence and justice warrant nations' taking some measures to collectively defend themselves and others against aggression.

Whether Christians or not, those who find the extreme pacifist and militarist positions untenable need ways to evaluate current and proposed military spending in terms of reasonable needs for national security. Unfortunately, it is now commonplace for leaders of nations to measure security in terms of the absolute size of their national military budgets or the share of their GNP devoted to military production. A moment's thought shows that this is a very misleading way to gauge a nation's security. Not only do nations face different degrees of risk, warranting different expenditure levels, but they also show varying degrees of wisdom in their allocations of military spending on research, force levels, and equipment for a variety of defense strategies. In this chapter we will show that an overemphasis on comparing national levels of military expenditure has diverted attention from analyzing the cost effectiveness of various weapons systems and from recognizing the economic impacts of increased defense spending here and abroad. Our aim will be to determine how to reduce the costs of defense while at the same time increasing national and world security. Some military spending is desirable, but at what cost do we spend increasing amounts on a defense system that may be ill-suited to meet the most realistic threats?

Since World War II, popular wisdom has maintained that military spending is good for the economy. After all, didn't the buildup of military spending prior to World War II virtually eliminate the devastating worldwide unemployment of the Great Depression? An alternative viewpoint was expressed by two early economists, Adam Smith and Jean-Baptiste Say. They lamented over the military spending of their own times, which diverted resources from the productive civilian sector to the unproductive—and even destructive—military sector. Say wrote, "Not only does [the soldier] fail to enrich society with any product, and consume those needed for his upkeep, but only too often he is called upon to destroy . . . the arduous product of others' work."[1]

These early economists remind us that the true economic cost of military spending is the need to forgo using human, material, and technological resources in ways that could otherwise supply people with goods to meet basic human needs. Worldwide, military spending in the early eighties equaled the entire income of 1.5 billion people living in the world's fifty poorest nations. The 245 billion dollars spent by the U.S. government in 1984 for military purposes was five times the domestic "poverty gap" (the amount by which the incomes of all poor American households fall below the official poverty line). Single items within these enormous budgets represent the sacrifice of other valuable goals. For instance, the price tag on a single modern fighter plane equals the cost of inoculating three million children against serious childhood diseases. And one hundred thousand working years of nursing care could be

1. Say, quoted by Olof Palme et al., in "Military Spending: The Economic and Social Consequences," *Challenge: The Magazine of Economic Affairs* 24 (Sept.-Oct. 1982): 6.

provided for what it costs to produce one submarine armed with missiles.[2]

The costs of defense today are huge, but projections are that the rate of growth of U.S. military expenditures will accelerate through the rest of the decade. Commitment to such systems as the Trident submarine and Trident II missile, the B-1 bomber, and the MX and cruise missiles will mean increased spending. Weapons procurement from 1984 to 1988 is expected to cost 380 billion dollars. (And typical cost increases of 100-200 percent make this an underestimate.) Previously restrained expenditures for military pay, maintenance, and spare parts will also rise. The magnitude of current military spending and its projected rise should raise serious questions about what kind of security we are buying and at what cost.

In this chapter we will first examine more closely recent levels and trends in military expenditures. This will prepare us for a look at whether the current direction of military spending is likely to accomplish its purpose—namely, to provide the United States with effective military security. We will outline budget cuts that would be made possible by a more realistic estimate of the risks involved. We will then move from the impact of current and projected military budgets on security to an assessment of their impact on domestic and foreign economies. In the end, we will be better able to choose what approach to military spending is likely to meet basic defense goals without endangering future economic or military security.

LEVELS AND TRENDS IN DEFENSE EXPENDITURES

Chart 1 and Chart 2 show what has happened to U.S. military spending over the past three decades and also show Defense Department projections of military spending through 1988. Chart 1 reveals that for most of the past thirty years, total real expenditures on defense (that is, expenditures with purely inflationary increases removed) have remained relatively constant at 170 billion dollars (in 1983 dollars), except for dramatic increases during the Korean and Vietnam wars. However, during the latter half of the Carter presidency and throughout the Reagan presidency, military expenditures have risen sharply. Currently they are at an all-time high for peacetime, and they are projected to rise above their previous two wartime peaks by 1986.

2. See Palme et al., "Military Spending," p. 5.

Chart 1. Department of Defense Outlays (fiscal years 1946-1982, projected 1983-1988)

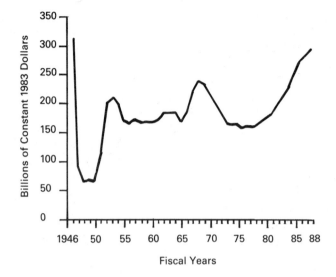

Sources: U.S. Department of Defense, Office of Assistant Secretary of Defense (Comptroller), unpublished data. Estimates for 1983 to 1988 from U.S. Department of Defense, Office of Assistant Secretary of Defense (Public Affairs) "FY 1984 Department of Defense Budget," Jan. 1983, adjusted to 1983 dollars.

Because the real GNP almost tripled over the past three decades, the share of military spending in the national economic pie fell from 10 percent during the 1950s to 6 percent during the 1970s—as Chart 2 indicates. However, projected budget increases will raise the military share of the GNP to 8 percent by 1986. We can appreciate some of the high levels and trade-offs involved by comparing defense spending with other categories of government expenditure. In 1985, defense accounted for 34 percent of all federal expenditures, three times the share allocated to health and equal to the combined shares allocated to Social Security and income maintenance.[3] Defense spending represents an overwhelming majority (about three-fourths) of all federal purchases of goods and services.

During the first three years of President Reagan's initial term of office (1981-84), the authorized defense budget grew in real terms by 31 per-

3. See Paul A. Samuelson and William D. Nordhaus, *Economics,* 12th ed. (New York: McGraw-Hill, 1975), p. 727.

Chart 2. National Defense Budget as a Share of GNP (fiscal years 1947-1982, projected 1983-1988)

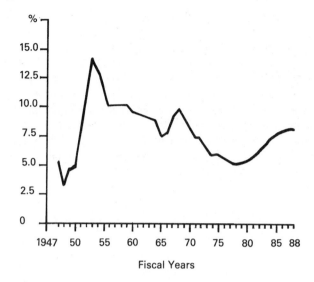

Fiscal Years

Sources: U.S. Office of Management and Budget, Budget Review Division, "Federal Government Finances," Feb. 1982, Table 12. Estimates for 1983 to 1988 from *Budget of the U.S. Government, FY 1984* (Washington: U.S. Government Printing Office, 1983), pp. 9-4, 9-53.

cent. In 1984 he asked Congress to accept a five-year plan that would further increase real expenditures by 22 percent by 1989.[4] In order to justify this buildup, the Reagan administration has frequently argued that the United States must dramatically increase military spending in order to close a widening spending gap between itself and the Soviet Union. In his 1981 State of the Union message, President Reagan said, "I believe my duty as President requires that I recommend increases in defense spending over the coming years. Since 1970, the Soviet Union has invested 300 billion dollars more in its military forces than we have."[5]

Given the enormous economic and political implications of attempting to close this alleged gap, we must evaluate the basis for claiming that such a gap exists. There are three serious problems with the much-cited "facts"

4. See William W. Kaufman, *The 1985 Defense Budget* (Washington: The Brookings Institution, 1984), p. 2.

5. Reagan, quoted by Franklyn D. Holzman, in "Myths That Drive the Arms Race," *Challenge: The Magazine of Economic Affairs* 26 (Sept.-Oct. 1984): 32.

which purport to show that the U.S.S.R. is now outspending the United States on defense at the rate of 50 percent, and that between 1971 and 1980 the U.S.S.R. outspent the United States by a total of 420 billion dollars (a figure that was updated since President Reagan's earlier speech).[6]

The first problem with these comparisons is the mistaken assumption that all Soviet defense spending is aimed at a potential confrontation with the United States. In fact, 20 percent of the U.S.S.R.'s defense outlays are aimed at defending itself against China (especially directed at maintaining a 750,000-person army situated on the Chinese border). The resources used to protect this flank have been drained away from alternative expenditures that would have better equipped the Soviets for a potential conflict with the United States. Furthermore, experts conclude that only 5 of the 20 percent of Soviet expenditures aimed at defense against China could easily be redirected to bolster a conflict with the West. Taking this into account reduces the 50 percent gap in current expenditures to 27.5 percent, and lowers the decade-long cumulative gap from 420 to 190 billion dollars.

The second major problem with the gap calculation is that it ignores the relative contributions made by Soviet and U.S. allies to their respective pools of common defense. This is no minor oversight, since U.S. NATO allies spent 95 billion dollars on defense in 1980, nearly *six times* what the Soviet's Warsaw Pact allies spent that year. When the correction for expenditures of allies is added to the correction for U.S.S.R. expenditures aimed at China, the menacing gap is *reversed* in favor of the United States by 480 billion dollars for the decade.

One further problem clouds the budgetary comparisons of U.S. and Soviet defense—namely, the difficulty of translating ruble figures into dollar amounts. Unable to get adequate information on ruble prices until recently, the CIA evaluated each component of Soviet military spending simply by putting a U.S. price tag on it. Thus, despite the fact that the Soviets pay their soldiers very low wages, the CIA took the *U.S.* annual cost of $20,000 per soldier and simply multiplied by the Soviet force size to get a figure for total Soviet defense spending on personnel. If Soviet leaders were to make the same error in reverse—comparing U.S. and Soviet military expenditures using only *ruble* prices—they too would get a frighteningly distorted picture. For example, multiplying the U.S. figures for military equipment by very high Soviet prices would make the annual procurement budget of the Unites States appear much more for-

6. The analysis that follows relies heavily on Holzman's "Myths That Drive the Arms Race," pp. 32-36.

midable than it really is. The reason? High-tech capital is generally much more expensive for the Soviet Union to produce than for the United States to produce.

Because the CIA now has many more ruble prices available, it should be reporting Soviet spending by simply taking the average of two calculations, one based on ruble prices and the other on dollar prices. Averaging the ruble and dollar figures, while also making adjustments for the U.S.S.R.'s border defense and its allies' expenditures, increases the military spending gap in our favor to 550 billion dollars. The logic of such averaging notwithstanding, the CIA is not following this more acceptable procedure in its public reports comparing U.S. and Soviet spending. However, in 1983 it did finally cut in half its previous estimate of the annual rate of increase in Soviet military spending since 1976—from 4-5 percent to 2 percent. (This revision suggests that the Soviet procurement budget during those years has not escalated but in fact has remained essentially flat.) Once the gap estimate is recalculated in light of slower recent Soviet spending growth, it rises by another 30 billion to 580 billion dollars in our favor.

This review of estimates comparing Soviet and U.S. spending does two things. First, it undercuts the very foundation of President Reagan's policy promoting rapid U.S. military buildup. The evidence on spending weighs heavily against the widely reported claims by the administration that since 1976 the Soviet Union has been engaged in a massive buildup of military hardware. Second, this review shows that emphasis on spending comparisons, even when accurate, tells us relatively little about the effective security levels financed by these expenditures. Quality can be at least as important as expenditure levels. It is generally acknowledged, for instance, that U.S. military equipment is of a better quality than Soviet equipment, and that the United States pays more attention than do the Soviets to training soldiers and to maneuvers.

Of course, some claims about Soviet military buildup are based not on spending estimates but on counts of equipment levels, warheads, and weapons systems. To the extent that the Soviets may have succeeded in such a quantitative buildup, despite much heavier spending by the United States and its allies, unwise allocation of U.S. defense funds and wasteful procurement must be blamed. For that matter, comparing hardware counts can be as misleading as making expenditure comparisons. If we suppose that one six-million-dollar Soviet tank can be put out of commission by one one-hundred-thousand-dollar "smart bomb," then it would be foolish for the United States to consider matching a Soviet tank buildup either tank for tank or dollar for dollar. If the alleged overall weakness of

U.S. defense exists despite superior funding, then it is clear that throwing *more* money into the same budget structure is a foolish and costly way to try to redress the situation.

OUR DEFENSE SPENDING—ITS IMPACT ON THE
LEVEL OF EFFECTIVE DEFENSE SUPPLIED

A detailed look at various components of the rapid increase in defense spending presided over by President Reagan turns up an interesting fact. Spending is not being guided by any basic reorientation in U.S. defense policy. Instead, "more of everything" seems to be the only message being conveyed by the defense establishment and supported by the administration.

Every year the joint chiefs of staff produce a list of the "minimum risk" capabilities needed to maintain the nation's security. Of course there is always a gap between the wished-for shopping budget and the amount that will be politically and fiscally acceptable. One approach to the resulting dilemma would be to force the chiefs of staff to go back to the drawing board to redefine ways of getting a maximum reduction of risk given the budget limitations. Instead, the administration uses the wish list of the chiefs of staff to press continually for budget increases.

Throughout this book we've emphasized the wisdom of counting the relative cost of various options rather than accepting a particular supply or level of performance as an absolute necessity for which the price tag is irrelevant. Unfortunately, the wisdom of counting costs does not appear to have been applied to military spending. The administration claims that we are currently vulnerable and clearly unable to honor agreements and treaty commitments to defend some forty nations. What it does not present or carefully examine is a comparison of a "minimum risk" force with less costly alternatives.

We should be getting answers to the question "What deployment of human resources and equipment will reduce the risks most economically?" For instance, is the greatest risk reduction (given feasible budgets) achieved by devoting spending increases to items useful for conventional warfare or to equipping forces for nuclear warfare? Like any other "improvement," every step closer to "perfect" security is more expensive than the last. Congress and the public need to be presented not with a single "minimum risk" option but with a variety of alternatives with various price tags, so that we can intelligently determine at what point going one step further toward "perfect security" simply is no longer worth the cost.

We will be considering a number of suggestions for reducing the costs of current and proposed defense budgets—proposals that do not compromise national security. However, before doing that, we turn to an important question: What is the likely security impact of a rapid buildup in defense spending, given that the increase is designed to fund "more of everything" rather than a carefully formulated new strategic plan?

THE PROBLEMS OF RAPID PROCUREMENT

It is in the acquisition of more hardware (weapons systems) that the greatest defense buildup is now occurring—in fact, this buildup is much greater than it was during the Vietnam War. Because important parts of this spending are heavily concentrated, involving a few major producers who are not able to expand production quickly, we can expect equipment prices to rise rapidly. There are, for instance, only a few plants producing forgings and pressed steel for airplane frames and landing gears. Furthermore, the most important materials for these forgings—like titanium, chromium, and cobalt—are imported from South Africa and Zaire, and are therefore subject to supply interruptions that would increase production costs.[7]

The potential for costly procurement bottlenecks is much greater in the area of defense than in any other area of the federal budget. Although a 20-billion-dollar increase in spending on defense procurement and military research and development represents only 1 percent of the U.S. GNP, it accounts for 10-20 percent of the output of major industries supplying defense goods. By contrast, the same dollar increase in government transfer payments, like Social Security and unemployment compensation, would be broadly distributed within the economy and thus have only a modest effect on the sales and prices of any particular industry.[8]

An appreciation for the magnitude of bottleneck problems can be gotten by comparing the defense spending buildup during the Vietnam War with President Reagan's projected increases. Early in the Vietnam War, the portion of the Defense Department budget devoted to equipment (as opposed to personnel) represented 7.9 percent of all goods production in the United States. When the buildup ended, this figure had risen by *a*

7. See James R. Capra, "The National Defense Budget and Its Economic Effects," *Federal Reserve Bank of New York Quarterly Review,* Summer 1981, pp. 29-30.

8. For data in this and the following two paragraphs, see Charles L. Schultze, "Do More Dollars Mean Better Defense?" *Challenge: The Magazine of Economic Affairs* 23 (Jan.-Feb. 1982): 32-35.

third, reaching 10.6 percent. In contrast, between 1981 and 1986, the Defense Department's share of all goods production is projected to almost *double*—from 5.9 to 10.0 percent. As a result, the claim defense will make on goods production for 1982-1986 is expected to be 30 percent of the total increase in nonagricultural production for the entire U.S. economy.

Such a rapid buildup in defense spending, concentrated in a few industries, will mean substantial cost overruns. Costs will exceed projections because rapid simultaneous expansion by several key producers simply bids up the prices they each must pay for technical personnel, materials, and equipment. (By contrast, a more measured pace of output growth is less inflationary, because input markets have time to respond to the increased demands made upon them.) Of course, under these conditions of "bottleneck inflation," actual additions of new military equipment are much smaller than budgetary increases imply. This poses a serious problem for national security. Substantial cost overruns will put increased pressure on the defense budget. The resistance Congress showed in 1985 to ballooning defense spending is likely to build as the administration seeks to cover rising costs of the same defense package. And history suggests that eventual cuts will be made at the expense of crucial defense categories like spare parts, training programs, standard equipment for conventional forces, and ammunition reserves. As a consequence, the cost overruns associated with rapid procurement may actually *reduce* U.S. readiness for combat. What we may end up buying is less security at a higher cost.

Unfortunately, it is politically difficult to avoid charging blindly into the problem just posed. There are two steps in the process of adding to defense expenditures: first, budget authority is approved by Congress; second, outlays are actually committed to contracts. Because the economic impact of congressional authorizations is usually not felt until two to three years after they are voted on, it is politically easy to accept funding for new weapons systems. When cost overruns for the new weapons and equipment eventually put pressure on the military budget, it is then politically easier for Congress to show its determination to "hold the line" by cutting authorizations for *non*-weapons expenditures, because these cuts have the political advantage of producing immediate budget relief. The alternative—canceling further procurement of existing weapons—would be difficult because it would amount to congressional acknowledgment that poor decisions and wasteful overspending occurred in previous budgets. U.S. security needs would be better served if Congress refused to grant authorization for some new weapons development,

TABLE 1

GROWTH IN THE BACKLOG OF DEFENSE AUTHORITY AT THE END OF EACH FISCAL YEAR
FROM 1981 TO 1985

Item	1981	1982	1983	1984	1985
Obligated authority	86.3	107.6	128.7	155.4	188.4
Unobligated authority	26.5	34.6	43.4	43.0	50.5
Total (in billions of dollars)	112.8	142.2	172.1	198.4	238.9

Source: Budget of the United States Government, Fiscal Year 1983, p. 9-9; Fiscal Year 1984, p. 9-11; Fiscal Year 1985, p. 9-16.

but such a vote would produce budgetary relief only two to three years later—beyond the decision-making horizon of some members of Congress and the administration.

The danger lurking in this political problem is illustrated by Table 1, which shows the growing gap between authorizations and commitments of budgetary authority between 1981 and 1985. By 1985, more than one-third of defense outlays became essentially *uncontrollable,* since the money had been approved but not yet spent.

A companion problem will further endanger national security if rapid buildup continues—namely, massive obsolescence. Many of the missiles, ships, aircraft, and tanks now being rapidly acquired will need to be replaced in about twenty years. Their replacement cost is expected to rise about two to seven times during that period, as greater technical sophistication is built into new equipment. When that happens, Congress will face an agonizing choice: to vote for the higher budgets needed to replace these items, or to vote for cuts (in combat forces, repair, etc.) that would seriously compromise national security.[9]

Given the momentum of the current and proposed defense budgets and the serious risks that rapid defense buildup poses to medium-term and long-term national security, we turn now to the question of what reductions in the defense budget are possible.

PROPOSALS FOR TRIMMING THE DEFENSE BUDGET

There are three specific ways budgets can be cut: (1) by reducing the duplication of systems supported by different military branches, (2) by slowing the pace of investment in new weapons, and (3) by eliminating

9. See Alice M. Rivlin et al., *Economic Choices 1984,* ed. Alice M. Rivlin (Washington: The Brookings Institution, 1984), pp. 70-71.

several costly programs with dubious objectives.[10] Let's review briefly the logic of each option. Unnecessary duplication of systems is obvious in strategic nuclear forces. The United States now has a nuclear force sufficient to meet the goal of responding to any Soviet nuclear attack with destructive and debilitating counterattacks that would prevent the Soviets from gaining any long-term advantages from such an exchange. Despite the adequacy of current forces (if modernized and maintained) to meet this objective, the Air Force is working on *five* systems to penetrate Soviet defenses: upgrading the B-52 bomber, producing two types of air-launched cruise missiles (ALCM-B and ACM), rapidly buying B-1 bombers, and working on big programs to eventually produce stealth bombers. Furthermore, the Air Force and Navy are also developing two very expensive ballistic missiles: the MX, a land-based missile, and the Trident D-5, a submarine-based missile. Experts have singled out the B-1 bomber and the MX missile as particularly superfluous. Eliminating them from the defense budget would have saved thirteen billion dollars in 1985 alone. Eliminating similar overlaps in expenditures for general-purpose forces would have reduced the 1985 military budget by another ten billion dollars.

We have already described the impact of rapid acquisition on weapons costs, as well as the problem of massive obsolescence and very high replacement costs twenty years later. All these costs can be reduced substantially by a more orderly approach to modernization. For instance, current capital equipment can be replaced at the end of its normal use-life. Thus, instead of rapidly replacing tanks with the latest model, the military would keep a tank with a 22-year use life in service for its full lifetime, and only then replace it with a next generation tank. A ceiling of 5 percent or less might reasonably be put on annual increases in the military investment budget. A more measured pace of acquisition would provide the added bonus of permitting better evaluation of proposed systems before they are chosen and put into place. Overall, slower procurement would have saved an estimated 3.1 billion dollars in 1985 alone, and savings would certainly increase in the longer run.

Finally, there are a number of costly programs that should be eliminated because their objectives are dubious. Of the numerous examples we could cite, we mention three examples that have been studied by defense experts at the Brookings Institution. First, rapid modernization of defenses against Soviet bombers seems unwise when Soviet ballistic missiles are the greater threat to our defense. Second, it is surely premature to

---

10. The following discussion draws heavily on Rivlin et al., *Economic Choices 1984*.

promote research on a leakproof defense against missiles (the "star wars" system) beyond the exploratory level. And third, given the great vulnerability of U.S. carrier battle groups, it seems unwise to have spent about eight billion dollars in 1985 to increase their numbers for possible use against Soviet naval ports. Savings expected by eliminating these and similar programs with questionable objectives would have added up to 18.7 billion dollars in the 1985 defense budget.

The grand total of money that would be saved by eliminating duplication, curtailing questionable projects, and slowing procurement was estimated at 45 billion dollars in 1985 alone. (To these savings there could have been added another 7.3 billion dollars in specific suggestions made by the President's "Private Sector Survey on Cost Control," the so-called Grace Commission report.) This would have amounted to a 15 percent reduction in the fiscal defense budget for 1985, with the largest reduction falling in the procurement account. The savings over five years would have added up to 175 billion dollars. Even a revised budget based on high-threat contingencies would yield a saving of 144 billion dollars over a five-year period.

The bottom line is that it is possible to make sizable cuts in our defense budget without weakening our defense posture. These estimates are not based on any assumption that we should trust the Soviet Union. They do not represent a "peacenik" budget but rather a more efficient Reagan budget. And making good on these savings now would leave the United States in a better political and economic position to meet future security needs.

DOMESTIC IMPACTS OF THE RISING DEFENSE BUDGET

Thus far we have undermined the alleged Soviet spending threat as a reason to rapidly increase military expenditures. We have pointed out the risk that embarking on rapid buildup poses to our national security. We have explained the wisdom and feasibility of cutting back the defense budget over a five-year period. We now turn to reasons for holding down the rate of defense budget growth that arise out of its impact on both the domestic and the world economy.

EMPLOYMENT EFFECTS

Popular opinion has it that defense spending is good for the economy. It creates more jobs, gives us a source of export earnings (since the United States ranks first in the export of military arms), and produces technological spin-offs applicable to manufacturing processes and products in the civilian sector. This popular opinion is well grounded in historical precedent. During the U.S. preparation for and participation in World War II, employment increased by eighteen million workers. And despite the fact that over one-half of industrial output went to the war effort, what remained was still greater than the total output for any year in the 1930s. The United States entered the war on the heels of the Great Depression and emerged with a newfound prosperity.

This experience was re-enacted, although less dramatically, during the Korean and Vietnam conflicts. The period of the Vietnam buildup in the 1960s was accompanied at home by the longest industrial expansion unmarred by a business recession in U.S. history. Employment, incomes, and productivity all increased rapidly.

Yet, despite these earlier fortuitous outcomes, it would be a mistake to conclude that today's defense buildup could achieve the same results. The previous developments were initiated in an economic environment quite different from that of the mid-1980s. During the earlier periods of military buildup, the U.S. economy was experiencing a high level of unemployment, an extremely low rate of inflation, and a balanced federal budget. The past fails to serve as a guide to the future for perhaps an even more basic reason: past military buildups were relatively short-term events with "light at the end of the tunnel." By contrast, the present buildup appears to be permanent, requiring recognition of the long-term as well as the short-term consequences of defense spending. In the remainder of this section, we will first examine the short-run impacts of defense spending on employment and inflation, then explore the long-run impacts.

Creating jobs for those seeking work is one of the highest priorities that a well-functioning economy can meet. From an economic vantage point, work creates needed goods and services and, along with these, a flow of income to workers. But just as important are the noneconomic benefits of work. Employment provides us with the opportunity to develop our abilities, to cooperate with others, to meet our obligations to family and community. In short, employment is an important source of human dignity and self-respect.

It is also obvious that spending—any kind of spending—will create jobs by increasing the demand for output. Military spending in the United States currently provides work for more than three million employees of the federal government, including two million on active duty, and at least two million more employed in private-sector businesses supplying goods and services to the military.[11] Yet, despite these impressive statistics, the net effect of military spending has probably been to *reduce* employment opportunities, especially for those who need them most.

The key question to ask in evaluating the impact of defense spending on employment is "How does military spending compare with alternative uses of the same money? Does it create as many jobs per dollar spent?" Phrasing the question in this fashion avoids the error of evaluating military spending in an unrealistic vacuum.

There are several reasons why military spending tends to create fewer jobs than an equal dollar amount of other types of spending. First, military spending requires more manufacturing and fewer service-type jobs than does nonmilitary spending. This means that the majority of a given dollar amount of expenditure goes for purchases of materials, not employment. Second, military spending employs a higher proportion of engineers, scientists, and managers than does manufacturing in general.[12] Because these occupations require a substantially higher salary per worker, a given expenditure employs fewer workers. Furthermore, those in job classifications most demanded by the military, like professional and technical workers, are those who least need additional job offers. For instance, the 3.7 percent unemployment rate for professional and technical workers in 1982 was about as low as possible given normal job turnover, whereas the rate for laborers and machine operators was a high 20.9 percent. Employment for this latter group is not greatly improved by military spending.[13] Finally, military spending frequently "employs" large quantities of sophisticated capital equipment. Dollars spent on equipment provide work for capital, not labor.

Because military spending provides fewer jobs per dollar (or per billion dollars) spent than do many other types of spending, one should expect employment to decline as federal budgets are shifted to favor defense spending. A recent detailed study of military employment in the United States proves the point. It estimates that in 1975 a billion dollars spent on defense would have created 76,000 jobs, compared with 80,000 jobs for a billion spent on health at the local level, or 104,000 jobs for a billion spent on education at that level.[14] Thus, if military expansion is

11. See Robert W. DeGrasse, Jr., "Military Spending and Jobs," *Challenge: The Magazine of Economic Affairs* 26 (July-Aug. 1983): 9-10.
12. See Table 8 in DeGrasse, "Military Spending and Jobs," p. 12.
13. See Table 9 in DeGrasse, "Military Spending and Jobs," p. 14.
14. See Palme, "Military Spending," p. 9.

accompanied by cutbacks in social services, as is the case today, the net effect is to increase *un*employment, not employment.

What would be the likely effects on employment if, instead of shifting dollars from other programs to the military, an arms buildup were financed with higher taxes? According to other studies, money redirected to military contracting through taxation would produce significantly fewer jobs than would money left in the private sector.[15] Consequently, taxing fifty billion dollars away from the household sector to increase defense would reduce employment by one and a quarter million people, causing an increase in the unemployment rate of about 1.1 percent.

We are currently financing a portion of defense increases with a shift away from other categories in the federal budget, but we are not raising the balance with higher taxes. What are the employment implications of deficit-financed military expansion? At first glance this would seem to have no depressing effects on employment, but first glances can be deceiving.

To avoid the potentially inflationary consequences of too much spending and an overheated economy, monetary authorities have tried to carefully restrict growth of the money supply, thereby raising interest rates. These higher interest rates affect employment on several fronts. Any interest-sensitive spending—including most business investment spending as well as household spending on new homes—drops quickly. So employment falls in the capital goods and construction industries. High interest rates also bolster the value of the dollar, penalizing U.S. export industries and increasing competition from foreign imports. Consequently, employment falls in agriculture, the textile and steel industries, and numerous other industries. In the long run, the costs mount because reduced business investment spending today slows U.S. productivity gains and the ability of U.S. business to compete tomorrow.

Recent studies of slow economic growth in Japan between 1894 and 1906 show that military adventurism drained badly needed resources from key economic sectors. The share of military spending rose from 3 percent of the GNP during the period from 1887 to 1893, to a high of 20 percent in 1905; and during a single year—1898—military spending accounted for 51.2 percent of central government spending.[16] All in all, it seems reasonable to conclude that in the United States today, as in Meiji-era Japan, the net effect of massive military buildup is slower economic

15. See the studies referred to by DeGrasse, "Military Spending and Jobs," p. 12.

16. See chap. 7 of Allen C. Kelley and Jeffrey G. Williamson, *Lessons from Japanese Development: An Analytical Economic History* (Chicago: University of Chicago Press, 1974).

growth and higher unemployment levels. In a later section, we will more fully address the consequences of rising military spending for U.S. economic growth.

Indeed, it appears that the trend toward job loss is getting worse due to the changing composition of defense spending in the 1980s. The most rapid growth is occurring in the areas of weapons procurement and research and development, which produce the fewest jobs per dollar spent and demand the highest skill levels. For example, defense employment in the United States accounts for 6.1 percent of all workers but employs 19 percent of all machinists, 22 percent of all electrical engineers, 38 percent of all physicists, 54 percent of all airplane mechanics, and 59 percent of all aeronautical engineers.[17] These are skill categories with essentially zero unemployment even in the absence of a defense buildup. Because of its biased requirements for skills already in high demand, defense spending today reduces total employment—perhaps more than it ever did before. The current buildup also serves to raise even higher the barriers to employment for workers having low skill and education levels, thereby worsening the problem of hard-core unemployment.

INFLATIONARY EFFECTS

Earlier we described bottleneck problems that result from rapid military procurement. These problems put pressure on the defense budget through rising prices. They jeopardize our national security because they eventually force decision-makers to institute budget cuts; they can also aggravate general inflationary pressures. Rapid military buildup for the Korean War, for instance, contributed to raising U.S. inflation rates from 1 to 8 percent per year; buildup for the Vietnam War was largely responsible for more than tripling previous inflation rates.

Two additional reasons explain why rapid military buildup is likely to be inflationary. First, the very process of procurement through military contracts makes for higher price increases in defense industries than elsewhere in the U.S. economy. Military contracts are written to cover production costs and provide a profit equal to a certain percentage of costs. Because producers' profits are thus guaranteed, there is very little pressure on contractors to keep costs down. Second, since there are often few producers of certain kinds of equipment and only one buyer (namely, the Defense Department), competitive pressures do not keep prices down. In fact, the rate of inflation in military industries is routinely much

17. See Palme, "Military Spending," p. 10.

higher than in the rest of the economy. For instance, between 1972 and 1980 the annual inflation rate for electronic equipment sold to the military was 6.6 percent, compared to only 1.6 percent for radio and TV receivers sold to consumers.

Unfortunately, higher inflation rates in defense industries tend to spill over into the rest of the economy when there is a rapid buildup in military procurement. In order to increase output, defense industries must hire more workers and buy more equipment. But because the number of engineers and supplies of equipment cannot increase very quickly, defense industries must bid for them against the private sector. As a consequence, labor and equipment costs are forced up in nonmilitary sectors.[18]

One final consequence of inflationary pressures induced by rapid military buildup is that some nondefense producers, when faced with rising labor costs, will meet the payroll by reducing investment. Lower investment levels mean slower overall economic growth, which itself is likely to be a direct consequence of rapid military buildup.

SLOWER PRODUCTIVITY GAINS AND WEAK ECONOMIC GROWTH

This may well be the most serious domestic consequence of rising defense budgets. The potential inflationary impacts of rapid defense buildup can be mitigated by tight monetary policy, as the mid-1980s show. However, the higher spending to pay for more defense combined with monetary restraint to keep inflation down has produced higher interest rates. In effect, the federal government has siphoned off private savings to pay for military expansion, leaving less money available to finance investments in plants and equipment for the civilian sector. Because investment is a key factor in economic growth, choked-off civilian investment portends poor future prospects for the U.S. economy.

We used Japan's slower growth at the turn of this century as an example of how costly military buildup can be. Data on the growth experience of industrial countries since World War II suggest that rising military expenditures have reduced investment in the production capacity of the private sector. Furthermore, countries like Japan and Canada, where military spending has been low, did a better job of weathering economic difficulties in the 1970s than did the United States and the United Kingdom, where defense spending represents a high share of the GNP.

It has frequently been claimed that military spending is good for an

---

18. See Palme, "Military Spending," pp. 11-12.

economy because defense research produces spin-offs useful to the civilian economy. The development of nuclear energy, electronics, and aircraft are examples of such spin-offs. However, one realizes after only a moment's thought that resources devoted to research and development for defense are resources that could have been used to develop technologies directly applicable to the civilian sector. The "miracle" of the economic growth and resiliency of Japan following World War II is not unrelated to the small size of its military industry (about equal to its toy industry) and to the miniscule share (only two percent) of publicly financed research devoted to defense. This contrasts sharply with the statistics for the United States and Great Britain, where *half* of all publicly financed research is devoted to defense. (It is worth noting, furthermore, that the most dramatic spin-offs of U.S. military research in electronics have been produced not in the United States but in Japan.) The United States and the United Kingdom have spent heavily on military research and allowed the share of the GNP devoted to civilian research to fall. By contrast, other industrialized Western nations have significantly increased the share of the GNP going into civilian research. In Japan, for instance, that share rose by a full 50 percent between 1967 and 1979.

National economic growth is particularly fed by investment and by research leading to new technologies. Thus, a continued buildup in U.S. military spending, which crowds out civilian investment and research, promises to handicap the U.S. economy now and in the future. As we've said earlier, slower economic growth severely undermines U.S. battles against unemployment, inflation, and poor competitive performance in trade. Together, these are among the heaviest costs that our economy will bear as a result of high and rising military spending.[19]

CONSEQUENCES OF U.S. MILITARY SPENDING FOR THE WORLD

So far, our counting the cost of higher U.S. military spending has focused on domestic impacts. We must now consider the larger context of worldwide impacts.

During the Reagan presidency, the United States has adopted a "get tough" attitude toward the Soviet Union, both in terms of direct competition between the two nations and in terms of upheavals in the Third World that are attributed to Soviet involvement. The Reagan administration justifies a rapid buildup in U.S. military spending by pointing to this

---

19. See Palme, "Military Spending," pp. 12-15.

perceived need for the United States to take a more determined stance vis-à-vis the Soviet Union. Unfortunately, the impact of higher military spending in response to perceived threats to our national security is likely to *aggravate* global insecurity. In this section we will trace the international consequences of higher U.S. military spending, from the purely economic impacts to those involving national and world security.[20]

Earlier we pointed to higher defense spending as the primary culprit pushing the U.S. federal budget into high and rising deficits. In the mid-1980s, these deficits forced up interest rates at home, thus serving as a magnet drawing savings out of other nations. The inflow of capital into the United States pushed up the dollar's exchange value, and this in turn adversely affected the U.S. economy on two fronts. First, U.S. export sales dropped severely because foreigners could not afford the higher dollar prices of our goods. Second, the U.S. banking system became more vulnerable because Third World countries that borrowed heavily during the 1970s (to meet development needs and to weather the shocks of higher OPEC prices) found it extremely difficult to pay the higher interest rates with more expensive dollars. Debt payments now encumber an increasing share of their export receipts. In fact, in 1984, one out of every five dollars earned by developing nations in export sales was needed to service their debts.[21]

Unfortunately, the U.S. response to these changes has been one that camouflages and aggravates the underlying problems. The United States has responded to its own sagging exports and rising imports—caused by an overvalued dollar—by raising trade barriers and aggressively pushing for lower foreign restrictions against U.S. products. Strong competition from imports has flooded the U.S. Trade Commission with manufacturers' petitions for tariff and quota protection. The number of such petitions filed in 1983 was triple the number filed in 1979. The commission has granted a number of these petitions, and thus the percentage of American products protected from foreign competition by nontariff barriers has risen markedly—from 20 percent in 1979 to 35 percent in 1983.

The discussion of trade in Chapter Eight highlighted the economic dangers of protectionist responses to trade problems. In a world economy that has become increasingly interdependent, U.S. attempts to protect itself from foreign competition quickly reduce the ability of foreign customers to buy U.S. exports. Furthermore, retaliatory moves by indus-

20. For a powerful development of this theme, see Robert B. Reich, "Towards a New Public Philosophy," *Atlantic Monthly,* May 1985, pp. 68-79.

21. See the World Bank's *World Development Report, 1983* (New York: Oxford University Press, 1983), p. 2.

trialized trading partners become more likely. Of course, strained trade relations with our allies do nothing to strengthen friendship and promote our joint security.

The impact of increasing U.S. protectionism is a much greater threat to the economic and political stability of Third World trading partners than it is to the economies of industrial nations. Poor nations already struggling to pay high interest rates on commercial debts—with expensive dollars—are harder hit than ever when U.S. markets are increasingly closed to their exports. It makes no sense for the United States to adopt a "get tough" stance toward debtor nations when increased protectionism prevents them from earning the very dollars they need to make scheduled debt-service payments. It is also *dangerous* for the United States to press debtor nations to adopt "austerity plans" (which lower their living standards) in order to meet their debt service obligations. Those nations politically unable to adopt these measures may thereby be forced to default, which would put serious strains on the international banking community. On the other hand, those nations that do adopt austerity measures may suffer serious social and political instability, playing into the hands of would-be "saviors"—whether rightist generals or Communists. Thus, high defense budgets can ultimately create greater instability in developing countries. Ironically, the U.S. response to threats of leftist pressures in several countries now beleaguered by debt problems has been to increase *military* aid.

We have come full circle. The push for more military spending in the United States creates economic tensions with our allies and contributes to the instability of Third World neighbors, both of which reduce our own national security. This state of affairs should make us pause to reconsider what we can reasonably expect to achieve with massive armaments and armies.

IMPLICATIONS AND CONCLUSIONS

We have counted the many costs of rapid increases in U.S. defense spending. The costs range from dimmed prospects for long-run economic growth to rising world tensions that ultimately threaten our national security. We've noted that a rapid pace of procurement that cannot be sustained in the long run may even lower the effective level of defense purchased with tax dollars. All these costs suggest that the types of defense budget cuts proposed earlier are well worth pursuing. A leaner and more slowly growing budget would permit better planning. It would force the military services to more carefully coordinate their activities so that the strategies they are pursuing would offer the greatest risk reduction per dollar spent.

Ultimately, further revisions downward in military budgets worldwide will depend on the quality of U.S. and Soviet leadership in arms limitation discussions. And their success will require concerted citizen pressure. Here, informed Christians can offer the economic and political evidence that weighs against heavy defense spending. It is particularly appropriate that we do so, because we attach special importance to the good the U.S. fails to do when one-third of federal dollars are spent on military defense. With the hands of Jesus, we Christians touch the poor in our midst and in remote corners of our world. With the eyes of the Creator, we see the earth's degradation. In the Spirit's power, we reach out to redeem men and women, drawing them into the family of God. Having counted the cost of relying on "horses and chariots," we are better prepared to look increasingly to the Lord God for our security, freeing many human and material resources that are desperately needed elsewhere.

Questions for Further Consideration

1. For centuries, thoughtful people have realized that the real cost of defense is the sacrifice a nation makes by spending less for other worthy purposes—education, health, income assistance, conservation, and so forth. The quotation from President Eisenhower at the beginning of this chapter vividly highlights the cost in words echoing Jesus' portrayal of the Day of Judgment. In your opinion, does the current division of federal expenditures—34 percent allotted to defense—constitute a morally acceptable balance between defense and other needs?

2. A lot of political hay was made out of an alleged gap in military spending between the United States and the Soviet Union. On closer scrutiny, the gap seems to have turned in favor of the United States. What can be done to counter weapons and spending comparisons that are so often used in misleading ways by both the United States and the Soviet Union to gain support for increased military spending?

3. Why does the myth persist that military spending is good for domestic employment and economic growth despite the preponderance of evidence to the contrary?

4. How do you evaluate the risk that a rapid buildup in U.S. defense spending may be economically or politically destabilizing for Allies and developing countries?

Recommended Reading

There are many good introductory economics textbooks that comprehensively teach economic principles and analysis. One paperback book that develops economic concepts by dealing directly with important public-policy issues is the seventh edition of *Economics of Social Issues* by Ansel M. Sharp and Richard H. Leftwich (Plano, Tex.: Business Publications, 1986).

Challenge: The Magazine of Economic Affairs is a readable and highly informative periodical covering such public-policy issues as poverty, trade, defense spending, inflation, aid for development, and competitive industrial structures.

A thoughtful evaluation of capitalism in the light of Christian faith and ethics is available in Robert Benne's *The Ethic of Democratic Capitalism: A Moral Reassessment* (Philadelphia: Fortress Press, 1981).

The U.S. Catholic Bishops have issued a pastoral letter, *Catholic Social Teaching and the U.S. Economy* (Lanham, Md.: University Press of America, 1985). In it they do a good job of presenting a biblically based "Christian vision of economic life" and also issue challenges for U.S. public policy based on Christian teaching.

A useful book for those who want to work with fellow Christians to implement justice in economic life is *Toward a Christian Economic Ethic: Stewardship and Social Power,* written by Prentiss L. Pemberton, a sociologist, and Daniel Rush Finn, an economist and theologian (Oak Grove, Minn.: Winston Press, 1985).

The best sources for up-to-date information on developing countries and U.S. policy toward them are two annual publications. The *World Development Report,* published for the World Bank by Oxford University Press, provides data on comparative economic conditions, projects future scenarios, and also deals in depth with one major development issue (like population, agriculture, the role of government). *The United States and World Development: Agenda,* published by Praeger for the Overseas Development Council, does an excellent job of evaluating and recommending U.S. policy toward developing countries.

A valuable resource for following and evaluating the public debate on federal taxation and spending is the annual Brookings Institution publication entitled *Economic Choices.*

For current data on the defense budget and analysis of priorities, the slim annual Brookings Institution publication called *The Defense Budget* is extremely useful.